jewish holiday songs for children

with dances and games for all seasons

by Rachel Buchman

Cover art by Susan Marsh.

To Harv – the only one to whom
my first book could be dedicated.

A recording of the music in this book is now available. The publisher strongly recommends the use of this recording along with the text to ensure accuracy of interpretation and ease in learning.

Visit us on the Web at http://www.melbay.com — E-mail us at email@melbay.com

MEL BAY®

Table of Contents

Introduction

This book is for anyone interested in bringing Jewish music into the lives of young children. It is for those already familiar with Jewish holidays, customs and languages, and those who would like to know more about them. The material was developed in the classroom, with children of many backgrounds, and in my home with our children. I've sung these songs with children in Hebrew schools, with Orthodox Jewish children, with children from inter-faith families and with non-Jewish children. In every instance the children were delighted by the songs, and they taught me something new about them. They were attracted, not only to the lovely melodies and lively rhythms, but also to the ideas in the songs.

In this book I hope to introduce you to the ideas that excite young children and to show you how you can take these songs and make them your own, modifying them for the children you are with. I have included some of my teaching techniques – ways to make the songs come alive through singing, dancing, clapping, acting out the songs, and thinking and talking about the meaning of the words. I have found that by engaging children's minds and bodies they learn more and derive greater joy from music.

Although I intend this book for both parents and teachers, in my notes I refer to classroom activities. This is purely for simplicity's sake – being a parent *is* being a teacher, so I needn't repeat everything in the context of the home. You'll see how to adapt it.

Consider this book a resource and a guide. There is a lot of material here, so dip into it when the time of year is right, rather than trying to absorb all of it at once. As you learn the songs you will find that their richness will teach you to sing them in new ways.

The songs will help Jewish children develop a strong bond to and love for their heritage, so that they feel that heritage as their own and as something that will grow with them. For children who are not Jewish these songs will be a loving introduction to Jewish holidays and customs. I want to share this music (as I have shared the music of many other cultures) because through music we can teach our children to respect, appreciate, and understand themselves and one another. Perhaps with that understanding they will be able to help bring peace to the world.

Most importantly, I know these songs bring happiness to children. So let's sing the songs!

The songs in this book come from many different sources. In most cases I have taken the original and tinkered with it, whether it be a folk song or a song composed by a known author. I've rewritten lyrics to suit young children, or translated lyrics so that our children will not be deprived of the meaning of the songs because they don't speak Hebrew or Yiddish. I've added activities, dances, and discussion topics to nearly all of them.

The songs have a spirit of their own which just needed someone like me to release it into the world of children. I initially began looking for songs because of a great need I felt as a teacher, parent and performer, for Jewish holiday songs that were appropriate for young children. I wanted songs that would be pleasurable for me to sing, that had the potential to be used for movement or discussion, songs with fine musical qualities and content. My search was fruitful; the songs presented here are only some of those I've found, and I'm always discovering new ones.

Not only must the song be right for young children, so must the way it is presented. The ideas in this book should help you use the songs you already know more imaginatively. For young children music is as magical and as compelling as a good story. You will have more to enjoy with them and teach them if you have a few good songs and dances up your sleeve.

Music Resources

I am indebted to those who collected and wrote these songs and to their publishers. Below is a list of the published sources I used and a corresponding abbreviation which will appear by the names of the composers and lyricists as they are listed in this book. Explore these resources; each of these books is a treasure trove of songs.

1. N.C.S.: *The New Children's Songbook,* compiled and edited by Velvel Pasternak; Tara Publications, Cedarhurst, N.Y., 1981.

2. S.C.: *Songs of Childhood,* selected and edited by Judith Kaplan Eisenstein and Frieda Prensky; published by The United Synagogue Commission on Jewish Education, N.Y., 1955.

3. S.W.S.: *The Songs We Sing,* selected and edited by Harry Coopersmith; published by The United Synagogue Commission on Jewish Education, N.Y., 1950.

4. T.J.F.: *A Treasury of Jewish Folksong,* selected and edited by Ruth Rubin; published by Schocken Books, N.Y., 1964.

5. Y.T.: *Yontefdike Teg, Songbook for the Jewish Holidays,* compiled and edited by Malke Gottlieb and Chane Mlotek; published by the Jewish Education Press of the Board of Jewish Education, Inc., N.Y., 1972.

The following book does not appear as an abbreviation, but is full of charming songs for young children that encourage the imagination and creative movement: *Apples on Holidays and Other Days* by Leah Abrams; published by Tara Publications, N.Y., 1989. The song "I Have Pajamas" (Kachol-Lavan) comes from this book.

A Word About the Translations and Transliterations

to help you sing these songs

I have translated most songs into singable and sensible English. In some cases this wasn't possible, so I've given a literal translation of the Hebrew or Yiddish lyrics, along with singable English lyrics. The transliterations enable you to sing in the original language and to teach children to do so. Singing in other languages is fun and teaches children an important lesson: though everyone's language sounds different (and often funny at first), the children who speak those other languages sing about the very things that English-speaking children do. The experience opens up their minds to the way other people do things.

Singing in other languages enhances memory skills, listening skills, and mother-tongue language skills, as well as oral coordination. Singing in other languages also gives children a sense of accomplishment. It is a great tool for introducing geography (which children can start learning as soon as they start looking at books), history and social studies.

Of course, it is best to sing a song in the language it was written in, for lyrics, rhythm, and melody are inextricably tied together and lose much in translation.

Pronunciation Key for Hebrew Transliteration

a.....as in father
e.....as in educate
i......as in machine
o.....as in shore
u....as in blue
ey.....as in grey
ch.....as in Johann Sebastian Bach
r........as in French (ie: frère), at the back of the mouth
ts......as in cats
ᵉ ....indicates a vowel sound that is very short, but distinct enough so that there is no slur of the consonants on either side of it.

Pronunciation Key for Yiddish Transliteration

(adapted from Uriel Weinrich's *College Yiddish*)

a.....as in father, but shorter
e.....as in educate
i......between feet and fit
o.....between dawn and done
u....as in book, but with slightly rounder lips
ay.....as in mine
ey.....as in grey
oy.....as in boy
ch.....as in Johann Sebastian Bach
r........as in French (frère), at the back of the mouth
ts......as in cats

Double asterisks ** mark lyrics that are best for singing. Since in many cases I've presented several versions of a song, the double asterisks will guide you to the singable lyrics!

Acknowledgments

I owe thanks to many people. I have learned songs from several sources and have tried to credit them all. If I missed anyone, I thank you for passing on such a precious thing as a beautiful song; through this book these songs will reach more children. For her patience, her guidance and advice, I thank the Rebetsn Lazaroff, Director of the Lower School at Torah Day School in Houston. Thanks to Hilary Mackie for her excellent suggestions on transliterating Hebrew. As always, heartfelt thanks to my colleague, Ruti Shechter. She has given me encouragement and inspiration, describing to me her memories of singing some of these songs as a child in Israel. I thank her for the many hours she took going over the Hebrew texts with me, and for taking an interest in the details of this project that went far beyond proofreading. Many thanks to Alan Rusonik, Director of Religious Studies at Temple Emanu El, Houston. He always took time out of his full schedule to answer my questions about religious law and practice. And many thanks to the Director, Shirley Burkom, and former Director, Barbara Gettinger, of the Becker Early Childhood Center of Temple Emanu El, where I teach music, for giving me the freedom as a teacher to experiment with my ideas in their classrooms.

Thanks to my beautiful children, Judith and Jacob. They helped with this project with their drawings, their critiques, their singing, and their patience with a mom who had to interminably "work on The Book."

As always, my greatest thanks go to my husband, Harvey, who supported me with his good sense and humor. He is a rigorous proofreader whose ear for and knowledge of language has brought the text of this book to a level of readability it never would have attained without him.

A recording of the music in this book is also available and highly recommended by the publisher. The singers on this recording are pictured above: from left to right (bottom row) Amit Weisgal-Lenski and Jacob Yunis; (middle row) Barak Shechter, Tomer Fishman, Ayelet Fishman, Aviva Weisgal, Avner Lenski, Rachel Buchman, and Judith Yunis; (back row) Liora Fishman; and (on shoulders) Leeshai Weisgal-Lenski.

General Notes About the Holidays

Jewish holidays, including the Sabbath, begin and end at sundown. Most are celebrated both in the home and at synagogue, and almost all involve eating special foods, singing songs, and saying particular blessings. On several holidays the requisite for celebration is to hear or read the story of that holiday. In some cases, such as Passover, the celebration in the home is the most important part of the holiday. All are occasions when family and friends come together and when hospitality is extended beyond the family and close friends.

The Jewish calendar functions on a lunar cycle, although a complete year approximates one solar year. Each lunar month has a name and each month there is a minor celebration for the new moon. (The words for 'new' and 'month' share a common root.) Jewish people often talk about how 'early' or 'late' the holidays are in any particular year because Jewish holidays fall out on different dates in the secular calendar each year. I have given the corresponding months in the secular calendar so that readers will be aware of the time of year for each holiday, and how the Jewish holiday relates to its season and to the seasonal culture of America at any given holiday time. The calendar begins with the New Year holiday, Rosh haShanah, which occurs in late summer or early autumn. Except for the fast day of Tisha Ba-Av, the Jewish holidays fall more or less within the school calendar. The holiday cycle includes three agricultural festivals that reflect the earliest origins of the Jewish people; farmers were just too busy and hot for holidays in the summer!

The seasons for these holidays were originally the seasons of the land of Israel, where the climate is a lot more like that of Texas than, say, that of New York or Poland. The land varies from desert to humid coast to rich-soiled plains, mostly a subtropical climate. Try making sense of Tu biShvat (Jewish Arbor Day), which falls out in January or February, the dead of an Eastern European or New England winter! Having lived in Texas for nearly ten years now, I understand the cycle of the Jewish calendar much better than I did when I lived on the east coast. (Tu biShvat corresponds closely with Texas Arbor Day!) As a consequence of moving south I have also come to appreciate the varied cooking traditions associated with the Jewish people of warmer regions. Previously the only proper *Shabbat* (Sabbath) meal I knew would include hot chicken soup and a hot meat dish. Now when our family comes down to Texas to visit from New York, they look askance at gazpacho for Rosh haShanah, pesto and pasta for Shabbat dinner, and meat cooked outside on the grill for Purim!

I have indicated what I consider the strongest aspect of each holiday – agricultural, historical, spiritual. Each holiday has a different origin and focus, each its own mood and beauty.

This pyramid consists of some of the singers on the companion recording. From right to left: (bottom row) Barak Shechter, Judith Yunis, Tomer Fishman. Middle row: Ayelet Fishman and Jacob Yunis. Top row: Leeshai Weisgal-Lenski.

Drawings are by the following artists:

Melanie Adelman,
Chanah Adler,
Molly Salitsky Daffner,
Rivka Elfezouaty,
Ariela Emery,
Basia Grinshtein,
Leah Klein,
Devorah Leah Lazaroff,
Daniella Lewis,
Naomi Pollack,
Mor Regev,
Yonit Tanenbaum,
Jacob Yunis, and Judith Yunis.

Shalom, Shalom (Hello, Hello)

שָׁלוֹם, שָׁלוֹם

a lively greeting in
a medium tempo

music by Ella Shurin
lyrics by Nacha Rivkin
(N.C.S.)

**TRANSLITERATED HEBREW LYRICS:

Shalom, shalom, shalom aleychem
Shalom, shalom, shalom aleychem
Shalom aleychem, aleychem shalom
Aleychem shalom uvrachah.

**LYRICS IN HEBREW :

שָׁלוֹם , שָׁלוֹם , שָׁלוֹם עֲלֵיכֶם ,
שָׁלוֹם , שָׁלוֹם , שָׁלוֹם עֲלֵיכֶם ,
שָׁלוֹם עֲלֵיכֶם, עֲלֵיכֶם שָׁלוֹם
עֲלֵיכֶם שָׁלוֹם וּבְרָכָה .

TRANSLATION OF HEBREW LYRICS:

(shalom means hello, goodbye and peace)
Hello, hello, peace to you all
Hello, hello, peace to you all
Peace to you all, to all of you peace,
To all of you, peace and welcome.

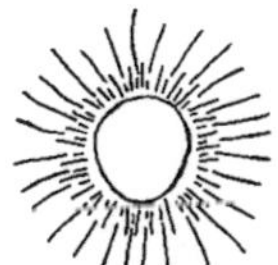

In Eastern Europe, Yiddish-speaking Jews greeted one another by saying, "Shalom aleychem" and responding, "Aleychem shalom." With slight variation, the greeting in Arabic is the same, "Salam Alekum" and it means the same thing: "Peace to you."

This is a nice song to start a singing time or to begin the day. I teach this song to children as an echo song. Be sure to pronounce that 'ch' with a strong sound in the back of the throat! The song works well acappella (without accompaniment). Here is how the echo works:

Shalom, shalom *(echo)*
Shalom aleychem *(echo)*
(repeat these two lines with echoes)
Shalom aleychem, aleychem shalom *(echo)*
Aleychem shalom uvrachah. *(echo)*

After the children know the song well, let them be the first voice and you be the echo. When the children are completely confident in their singing, let one of them be the first voice, the rest the echo, and you (the adult) don't sing at all!

To add to the fun, and to add an element of hand-eye coordination while singing, use hand motions to go with each line of singing. Here are the hand motions I use, but feel free to make up your own.

Shalom, shalom *(echo)*
wave right hand
Shalom aleychem *(echo)*
wave left hand
(repeat these two lines with echoes and motions)
Shalom aleychem, aleychem shalom *(echo)*
shake hands with yourself
Aleychem shalom uvrachah. *(echo)*
open arms as if to give a big hug, then draw your arms toward your chest, as if welcoming people in

Rosh haShanah

רֹאשׁ הַשָּׁנָה

Holiday:

Rosh haShanah: (Jewish New Year, in September or early October)

What's it about?

A spiritual and philosophical holiday, it is both festive and solemn. It celebrates the creation of the world, or the world's 'birthday,' as well as our own spiritual renewal each year.

How is it celebrated?

Synagogue services are held in the evening when the holiday begins and in the morning and early afternoon of the following one or two days. (The length of the holiday depends on which type of Jewish religious service one attends.) The most stirring part of the service is the blowing of the *shofar,* or ram's horn, which is repeated at intervals as part of the morning service. It is an irresistible call to the congregation to take stock of their lives, their relationships, and their actions. At home, after services, family and friends eat a festive meal. Apples are dipped in honey to represent a sweet new year; round *challah* (ceremonial bread) symbolizes the continuity of one year leading into another. Honey cake is eaten for a sweet new year.

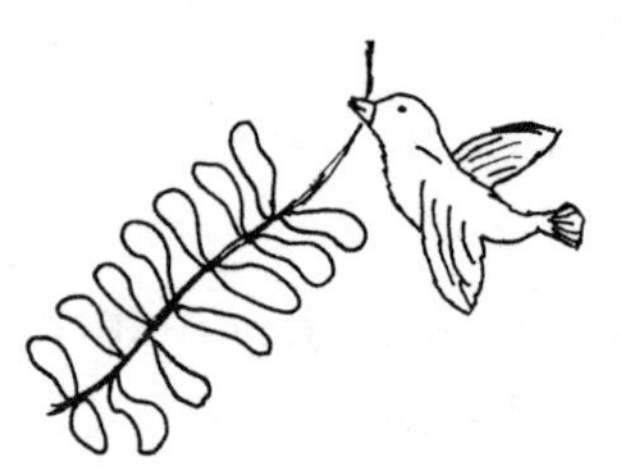

Tapuchim uDvash (Apples and Honey)

תַּפּוּחִים וּדְבַשׁ

American Jewish folk song
English lyrics by Rachel Buchman
Happy Valley Music, BMI
(N.C.S.)

medium slow,
with anticipation of
the New Year

C Am
Dip ap - ples in the hon - ey

Dm G7 C C Am
for a sweet New Year. Ta - pu- chim u - dvash l^{e} -

Dm G7 C F
Rosh ha - Sha - nah. Sha - nah to - - -

G7 C Am
vah, sha - nah m^{e} - tu - kah, Sha -

F G7 C
nah to - - - vah, Sha - nah m^{e} - tu -

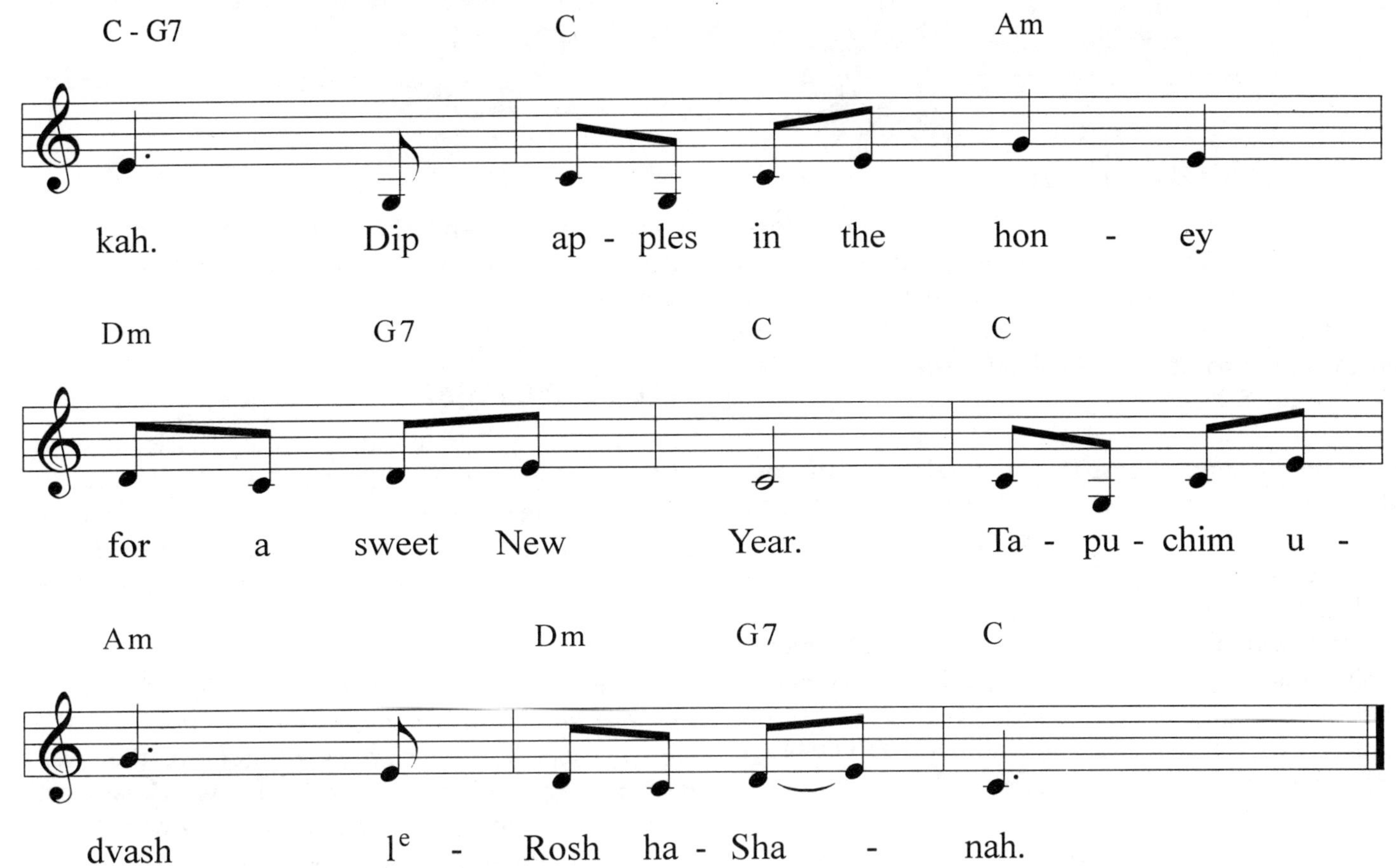

**Dip apples in the honey for a sweet New Year.
Tapuchim udvash leRosh haShanah.
Shanah tovah, shanah metukah
Shanah tovah, shanah metukah.
Dip apples in the honey for a sweet New Year.
Tapuchim udvash leRosh haShanah.

**TRANSLITERATED HEBREW LYRICS:

Tapuchim udvash leRosh haShanah,
Tapuchim udvash leRosh haShanah.
Shanah tovah, shanah metukah,
Shanah tovah, shanah metukah.
Tapuchim udvash leRosh haShanah
Tapuchim udvash leRosh haShanah.

**LYRICS IN HEBREW:

תַּפּוּחִים וּדְבַשׁ לְרֹאשׁ הַשָּׁנָה,
תַּפּוּחִים וּדְבַשׁ לְרֹאשׁ הַשָּׁנָה.
שָׁנָה טוֹבָה, שָׁנָה מְתוּקָה,
שָׁנָה טוֹבָה, שָׁנָה מְתוּקָה.
תַּפּוּחִים וּדְבַשׁ לְרֹאשׁ הַשָּׁנָה,
תַּפּוּחִים וּדְבַשׁ לְרֹאשׁ הַשָּׁנָה.

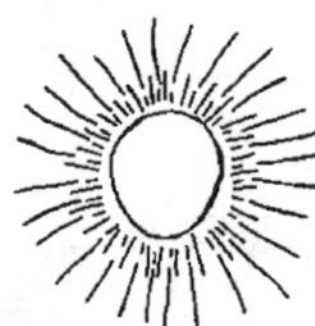  

Discussion Topic:

Before I sing this song with very young children (ages 1-4) I act out cutting up apples for the ceremonial apples and honey. Then we act out the song. When you sing the word *rosh* put your hand on your head, for *rosh* means head in Hebrew. Rosh haShana literally means 'the head of the year.'

In the simple sense it is the forefront of the year, but this also indicates what part of us should led us in our decisions and our actions. This is a theme which children can understand. We should not allow ourselves to be lead by strong emotions, which often happens. During Yom Kippur we pay particular attention to this weakness and to other human failings. We must develop our understanding and let that part of us (symbolized by the head, the thinking part) lead our ever-errant hearts and bodies.

When I act out the song with children I sometimes put the wrong hand on my head – the one that dipped the apple in honey! The children love these make-believe slapstick jokes.

This is a good time of year to introduce some Hebrew vocabulary, such as the words for apples *(tapuach-s., tapuchim-p.)* and for honey *(d[e]vash)*, for tree (*eyts* - from which the apples come), and other parts of the body besides the *rosh* (head). The beginning of the school year when we learn the story of creation is a wonderful time to talk and learn about the wonders of the earth and to remind ourselves that we must take care of and respect our planet and all her plants and creatures.

More Songs:

"All Things Bright and Beautiful," music adapted by Dr. Martin Shaw; *"Ruach, Ruach"* (an Israeli folk song with European origins), about apples falling from trees. The title means "Wind, Wind," which is also the Hebrew word for the spirit of God in the first verses of *Bereshit (Genesis).*

Another song for this time of year is *"Yismechu haShamyim."* In this song, every time you sing the words *hashamyim* (which means 'the sky' or 'the heavens'), ask the children to reach up high with imaginary paint brushes and paint the sky, as if they were God's helpers during creation, adding color to the world where first there was none. Children love to talk about colors, so ask them what their favorites are and ask them to look at the sky at different times of day and tell you what colors they see. This kind of discussion helps children become more aware of the beauty in the world around them. Remind them and their parents to notice it. The second half of this song is about the roaring of the sea, so when you sing *'yiram hayam'* ('let the sea roar') bring your hands together in a circular motion to climax in a clap, like a big crashing wave.

I Can Bake a Honey Cake

by Levi and Deutsch
from "So We Sing"

happily, in a medium tempo
(on recording sung in Bb)

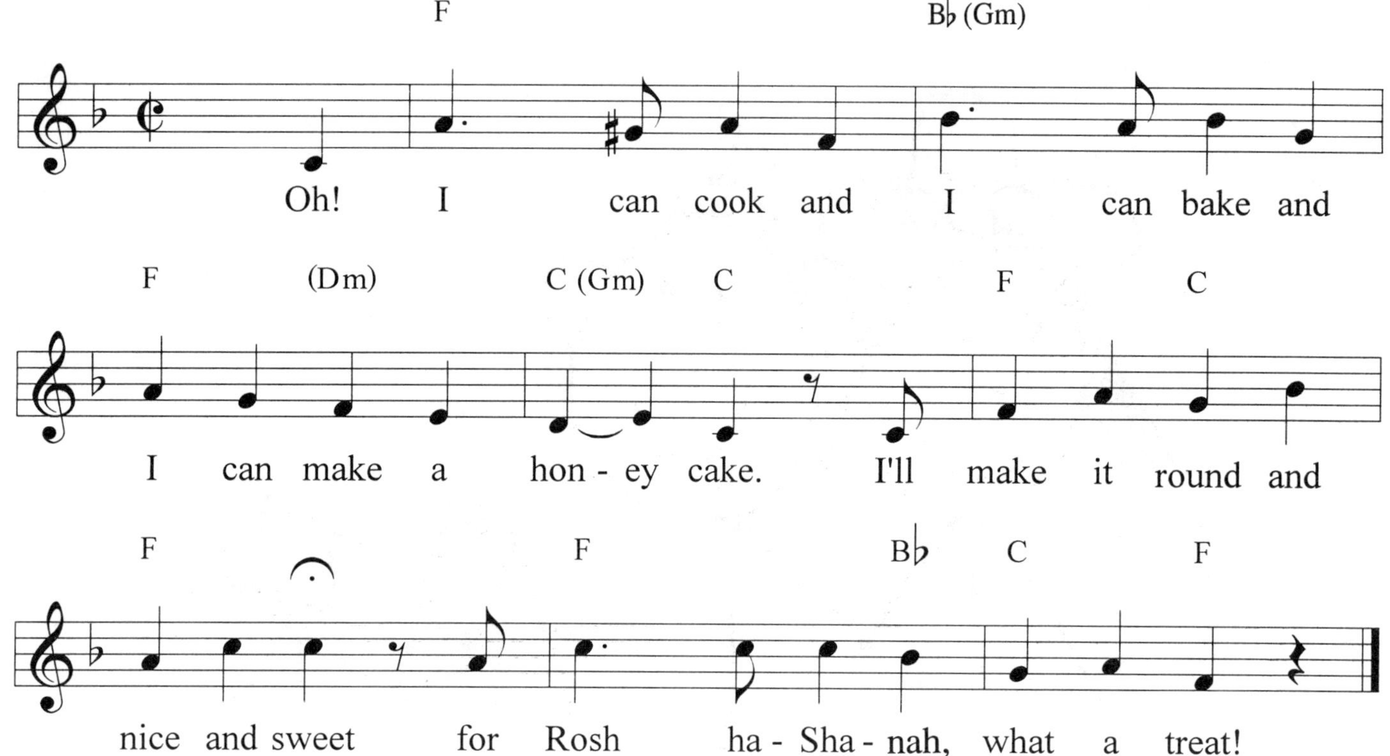

Oh, I can cook and I can bake
And I can make a honey cake.
I'll make it round and nice and sweet
For Rosh haShanah, what a treat!

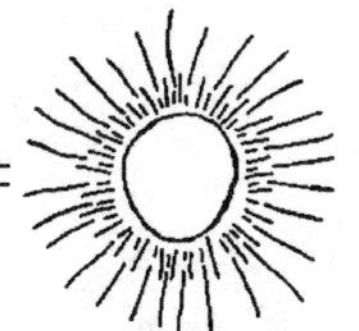  

This song is fun to act out, too. Add hand motions to each line as follows or make up your own:

Oh, I can cook
point proudly to yourself with right hand
And I can bake
point proudly to yourself with left hand
And I can make a honey cake
stir a big bowl of batter
I'll make it round* and nice and sweet
make a large, round motion with arms
For Rosh haShanah, what a treat!
gesture carrying the cake on a tray and offering to friends

Make believe you are sharing round the cake and say, *"Shanah Tovah!"* (literally - good year, meaning happy new year). Talk about who will celebrate the holiday with the children. If many guests are coming we'll need to bake a bigger cake. Sing the song again, this time exaggerating all the actions, to bake a huge cake. When you present it to the children to share this time, make it so heavy that all the children have to stand up to help carry it. If the children know how to take a joke, make the cake so heavy that you all drop it! Oh no! You'll have to sing the song again to bake a new cake!

*Ask the children to tell you the things they know that are round. With older children talk about the difference between drawing a circle and drawing a straight line. This is a symbol for the more philosophical ideas behind the new year celebration. In Judaism there are both circular and linear qualities of time, for as we repeat the holiday cycle we want each repetition to be made by a better person, by a better society.

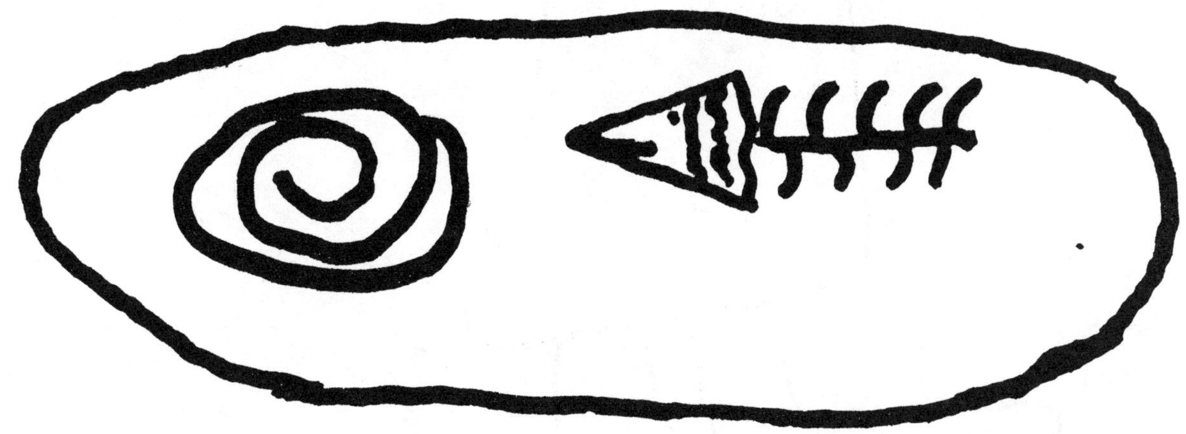

Yom Kippur

יוֹם כִּפּוּר

Holiday:

Yom Kippur: (Day of Atonement, in September or October)

What's it about?

A spiritual and philosophical holiday, it is the conclusion of the Ten Days of Awe which begin with Rosh haShanah. It is a holiday in which people examine their behavior, admit mistakes, and make plans to improve themselves. Prayers are said for a good year, a healthy, safe year, and it is a time when one is most aware of the fragility of human existence. One of the most important themes of the holiday is to apologize to those we have wronged. Friendship, repentance and trying harder to do the right thing are all themes children can relate to.

How is it celebrated?

The holiday begins in the evening with a service called Kol Nidre, the most solemn, introspective, and, many say, the most beautifully chanted of all holiday services. This is also when the fast of Yom Kippur begins. The next day synagogue services last for most of the day, while people fast from sundown to sundown. It is a quiet, contemplative day. The service concludes with a long blast of the *shofar.* The fast is broken with family and friends, and there is a feeling of renewal, a readiness to begin the new year with a clean slate.

Let's Be Friends

by Jackie Weissman Silberg
Miss Jackie Publishing, BMI

happily
(This is sung a little differently on
my recording than it appears here)

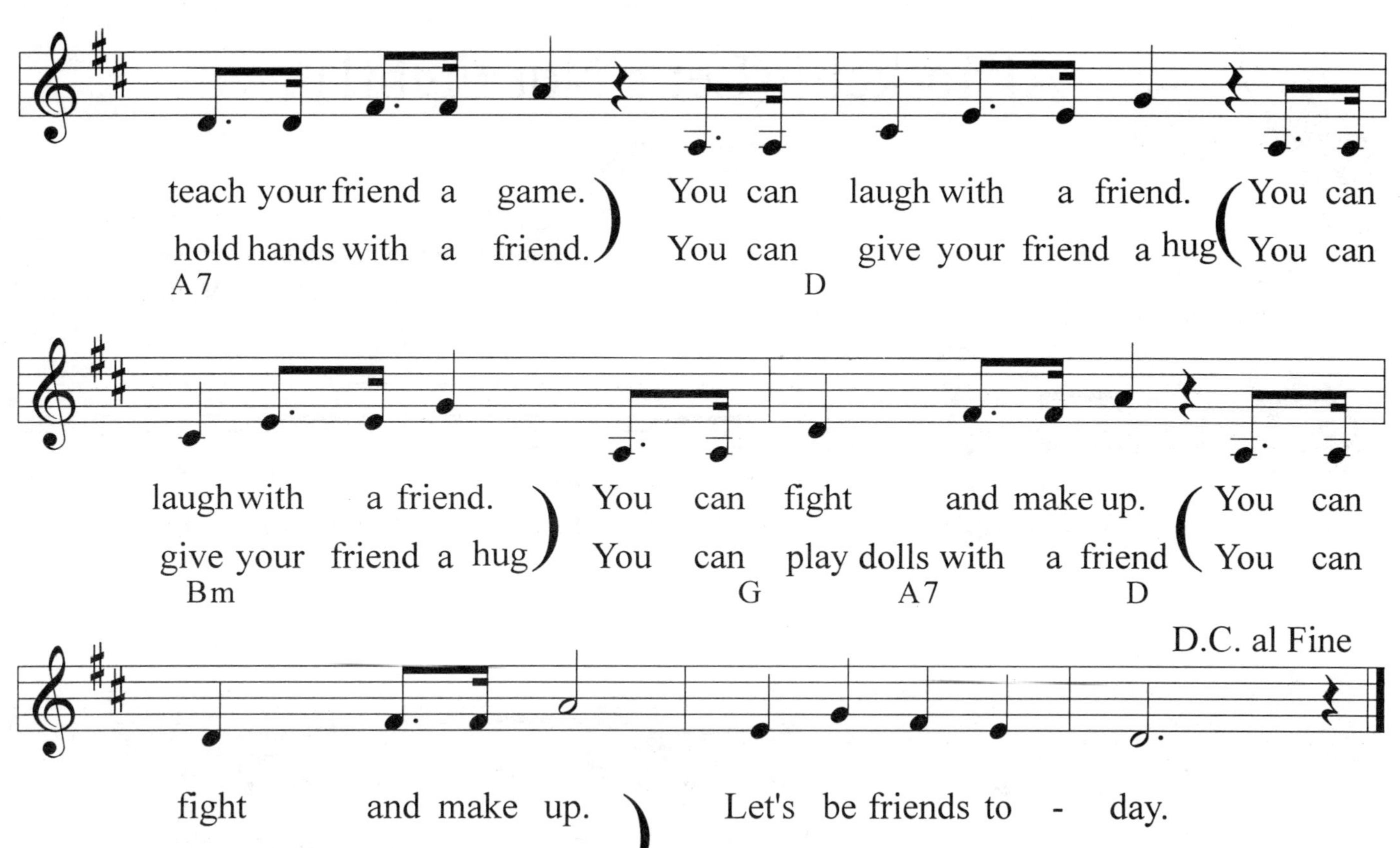

Chorus Let's be friends with one another,
Let's be friends with one another,
Let's be friends with one another,
Let's be friends today.

(Let the children give you suggestions; here are the suggestions the kids on the album gave me.)

You can teach a friend a game *(echo)*
You can laugh with a friend *(echo)*
You can fight and make up *(echo)*
Let's be friends today. *Chorus*

You can hold hands with a friend *(echo)*
You can give your friend a hug *(echo)*
You can play dolls with a friend *(echo)*
Let's be friends today. *Chorus*

(Let the children give you suggestions for what to do with a friend if your friend gets hurt.)

Discussion Topic:

Of all the themes of Yom Kippur, probably the best one to talk about with children is that of getting along with our friends. It is a theme that they can easily understand and one that is reiterated throughout the year. Because of the way the Jewish holidays fall out in relation to the school calendar, Yom Kippur is right at the beginning of the school year and is an excellent time to start talking about this subject.

More Songs:

Some other appropriate songs for Yom Kippur are the African-American spiritual, "Who Did Swallow Jo-Jo-Jonah?" (because the *Book of Jonah* is read in synagogue on the afternoon of Yom Kippur and one of its strongest themes is taking care of one's fellow man) and the funny Woody Guthrie song, "Don't You Push Me," which is full of real life situations between friends when they play and don't get along well.

Al Ta-keh! (Let's Not Fight!)

אַל תַּכֶּה!

**Let's not fight! It's not right!
Take my hand, left and right.
Chaverim tovim niyeh,
What good friends we all shall be,
Chaverim tovim niyeh,
What good friends we all shall be.

**TRANSLITERATED HEBREW LYRICS:

Al ta-keh! Zeh lo na-eh!
Ten li yad, v[e]od achat.
Chaverim tovim niyeh,
Chaverim tovim niyeh.

**LYRICS IN HEBREW:

אַל תַּכֶּה! זֶה לֹא נָאֶה!
תֵּן לִי יָד וְעוֹד אַחַת.
חֲבֵרִים טוֹבִים נִהְיֶה,
חֲבֵרִים טוֹבִים נִהְיֶה.

Here is a dance you can do:

Hold hands in a circle. (With older children, age four to five and up, count off partners; with younger children have them do the following actions without turning a particular way.)

turn to your partners, wag your finger at each other and sing:

Let's not fight!

turn the other way, wag your finger at each other and sing:

It's not right!

take hands in a circle (Older children can take hands with their partners, circling in their places. Younger children should join hands in a big circle with everyone.)

Take my hand, left and right.

circle around to the right

What good friends we all shall be!

circle to the left

What good friends we all shall be!

Repeat last two lines. Drop hands and repeat the song from the beginning.

(Repeat using the Hebrew lyrics, following the same pattern)

Star Jewish Pitcher
1955-66
(World Series 1963,'65-66
did not pitch on Yom Kippor
Oct. 6, 1965 in
World Series)
Sandy
Koufax

Sukkot

סֻכּוֹת

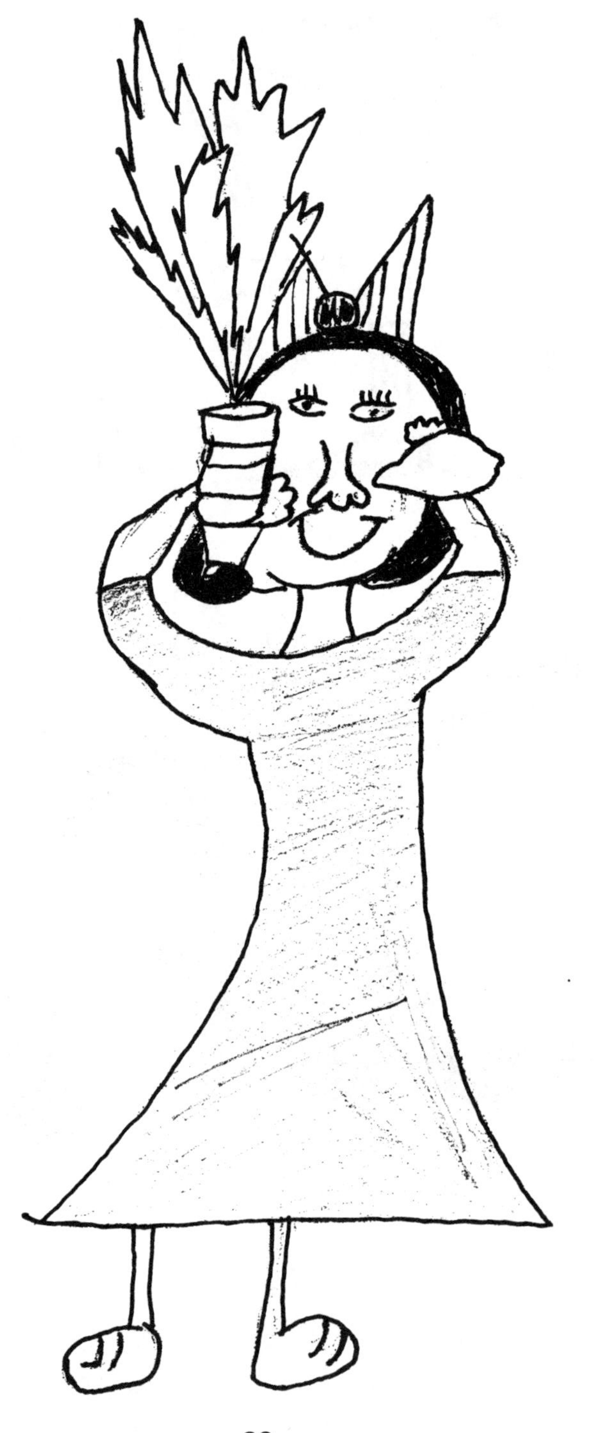

Holiday:

Sukkot (Feast of Booths, in September or October)

What's it about?

An agricultural and historical holiday. It is the Jewish harvest festival and it recalls the time when the Children of Israel crossed the desert in their escape from slavery and dwelt in temporary structures. It is a happy holiday tinged with the recognition of life's uncertainty. It is a holiday that celebrates the bounty of food and blessings people have and that encourages us to share that bounty with others. Hospitality and generosity are both themes of this holiday.

How is it celebrated:

People build *sukkot* (plural for *sukkah* in Hebrew), or booths (tabernacles), temporary structures, in their backyards in which they eat, sing, pray and sometimes sleep. The *sukkah* has a roof made of branches with green leaves, through which one is supposed to be able to see the sky. If it rains on Sukkot you get wet! The structure is traditionally decorated with fruits and vegetables. At the beginning of Sukkot there is a full moon; how nice it looks when seen through those green branches. Synagogue services are held. At these services there is a special ritual involving three types of branches bound together (called a *lulav)* and shaken along with a citron (a lemon-like fruit called an *etrog* in Hebrew). The significance of these rituals are rich and varied. At the synagogue there is usually a *sukkah,* too, in which all can eat and sing together. After services people feast and sing together at the synagogue or at home with friends and family.

Interdisciplinary ideas:

Art:

Have the children bring in a large box from home and let them each make and decorate a *sukkah* for their favorite dolls or stuffed animals. Get a large box (from a refrigerator or washing machine delivery) and make it into a classroom *sukkah* in which the kids can take turns eating and making their own little celebrations.

Literature:

Sholom Aleychem's stories, "Really a Sukkah" and "The Etrog," are both to be found in his book of short stories called *Holiday Tales,* translated by Aliza Shevrin. These stories are full of irony and the details of shtetl life. Read in their entirety they are excellent for older children. For younger children you might have to skip some of the descriptive passages. In either case the stories are well worth the effort and remain among the liveliest literature there is.

Social Studies:

Talk about other holidays similar to Sukkot, such as Thanksgiving (the idea of harvest, giving thanks, relief after a struggle – it is never easy to have a good harvest, our plenty is fragile. We depend on rain, sunshine, good seeds, and so on). Children are capable of and enjoy talking about these ideas if you introduce them with words they understand.

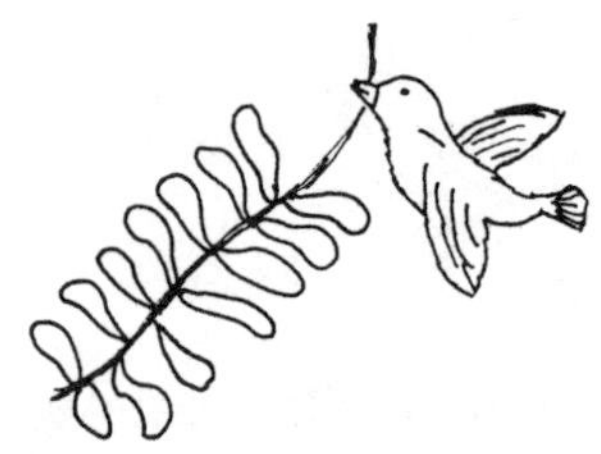

A Su-ke! A Su-ke!
(A Sukkah! A Sukkah!)
אַ סכּה! אַ סכּה!

joyfully and not too fast

music by Malke Gottlieb
lyricist unknown
English lyrics and finger game by Rachel Buchman
(Y.T.)

Am

A suk - kah! A suk - kah! Three
A su - ke! A su - ke! Dray

Dm E7 E

walls, a door, a roof, A suk - kah! A
vent, a tir, a dach, A su - ke! A

Am E Am-E7

suk - kah! With fresh green bran - ches hung, A
su - ke! Mit fri - shn, gri - nem s'chach, A

Am Dm

suk - kah! A suk - kah! Three walls, a door, a
su - ke! A su - ke! Dray vent, a tir, a

E7 E

roof, A suk - kah! A suk - kah! Where
dach. A su - ke! A su - ke! Mit

*Freely improvise with syllables

**A Sukkah! A Sukkah!
Three walls, a door, a roof,
A Sukkah! A Sukkah!
With fresh, green branches hung.
A Sukkah! A Sukkah!
Three walls, a door, a roof,
A Sukkah! A Sukkah!
Where happy songs are song!

Chorus: Lay, day, day...

**TRANSLITERATED YIDDISH LYRICS:

A Su-ke! A Su-ke!
Dray vent, a tir, a dach,
A Su-ke! A Su-ke!
Mit frishn, grinem s'chach.
A Su-ke! A Su-ke!
Dray vent, a tir, a dach,
A Su-ke! A Su-ke!
Mit frishn, grinem s'chach.

Chorus

**LYRICS IN YIDDISH:

אַ סוכּה! אַ סוכּה!
דרײַ װענט אַ טיר, אַ דאַך,
אַ סוכּה! אַ סוכּה!
מיט פרישן, גרינעם סכך.
אַ סוכּה! אַ סוכּה!
דרײַ װענט, אַ טיר, אַ דאַך,
אַ סוכּה! אַ סוכּה!
מיט פרישן, גרינעם סכך.

צוזינג

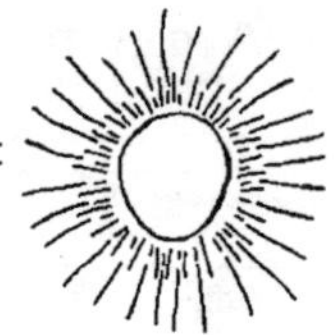  

With younger children, act out the song this way:

A Sukkah! A Sukkah!
Three walls,
show three fingers for '3 walls'
a door,
hide your face behind flat hands for 'a door' – then open the hands, as though playing peek-a-boo
a roof,
Fold arms and hold them away from the body to make a roof. There should be space between the arms to show the space between branches on a sukkah roof.

Musical Activity:

During the chorus, have the children clap their hands or play percussion instruments (tambourines sound particularly good with this song). Be sure they wait to play until the chorus begins. Sing the verse slightly slower and smoother and quieter than the chorus section, so that when the latter comes, the children can hear and feel the change in tempo (speed), dynamics (loud or quiet), and energy.

This game teaches them to use percussion instruments in a disciplined manner and develops their sensitivity to changes in feeling, whether in music or in the way a person speaks or tells a story. It shows them how they can create a sense of anticipation and suspense, how much they enjoy the release of that suspense when they start the chorus.

Encourage the children to play their instruments or clap and sing at the same time. This is a developed skill which becomes more sophisticated the older children get and the more they practice combining the two activities.

Great Big Stars

African-American spiritual

Great big stars, 'way up yonder
Great big stars, 'way up yonder
Great big stars, 'way up yonder
Oh, my little soul is gonna' shine, shine.
Oh, my little soul is gonna' shine, shine.

Great big moon, 'way up yonder
Great big moon, 'way up yonder
Great big moon, 'way up yonder
Oh, my little soul is gonna' shine, shine.
Oh, my little soul is gonna' shine, shine.

Discussion Topic:

This song has an almost magical calming effect on children (and adults!). I've seen it soothe even hyperactive children or those who have difficulties concentrating. It is a wonderful song to sing after a lively one or after a dancing session. It is a perfect song to begin rest period or to end a busy day.

This song beautifully illustrates the injunction to see the stars though the roof of the *sukkah*. The structure should not cut us off from the natural world, nor protect us too much from it. The fragility of the *sukkah* is a symbol of the fragility of our lives.

Talk about the difference between things in the sky that people create and those things we cannot. Even two-year-olds can engage in this discussion. It awakens their sense of wonder in the natural world, and stimulates their thinking about the world beyond their classroom. When a child said to me, "You can make a bird, Rachel, you can draw a picture!," it was a challenge to clarify the difference between the bird I can create and the one that flies in the sky.

When singing the song for Sukkot, substitute for 'great big stars' other things in the sky which people cannot create. Go as far as you can with this, including planets and solar systems, comets and meteors. Children at a very young age are learning about the universe and will be able to make these suggestions. If they can't it is a great opportunity to introduce them to the great beyond. Then there is the ever beloved thunder and lightning, rainbows and butterflies, and the occasional flying horse! When singing the song at other times of the year, let the children substitute anything they see up in the sky (airplanes, balloons, and so on) and help them understand that they might create something one day that can go up into the sky.

Simchat Torah

שִׂמְחַת תּוֹרָה

Holiday:

Simchat Torah (Rejoicing in the Torah, in October)

What's it about?

A spiritual holiday. It marks the end and new beginning of the cycle of reading the Five Books of Moses each year. It celebrates not only the literal *Torah* which is the Five Books of Moses, but the *Torah* in the greater sense of the word, which includes the other books of the *Tanach* (Bible), the teachings of the Rabbis, the commentaries on the *Torah*, and Jewish learning, in general. This holiday ends the cycle of fall holidays, beginning with Rosh haShanah, which quickly follow one after the other for more than three weeks.

How is it celebrated?

There is a special ceremony in synagogue marking the end of one year's cycle of *Torah* reading and the beginning of a new cycle. Special prayers are said; songs are sung while there is a parade in the synagogue in which the *Torot* (plural for *Torah* in Hebrew) are carried through the congregation. There is dancing, and children wave decorated flags and eat treats, such as candy and candied apples.

Degel Tov (Will You Be My Flag?)

דֶּגֶל טוֹב

American Jewish folk song
English lyrics, chorus, game by Rachel Buchman,
Happy Valley Music, BMI
2nd half of Hebrew verse by Liora Fishman and Ruth Shechter
(N.C.S.)

a walking tempo, happy

C F

Will you be my flag to - day? Will you be my
De - gel, de - gel, de - gel tov, De - gel tov she -

G C

flag? Will you be my flag to - day
li, Bo tir - kod, tir kod i - ti

F G C F C

on Sim-chat To - rah? (Chorus:) La, la - la, la - la (clap) la - la!
be- Sim-chat To - rah.

F C F C G7 C

La, la la, la la la, La, la - la la - la (clap) la-la! La, la - la la la la.

**Will you be my flag today?
Will you be my flag?
Will you be my flag today,
On Simchat Torah?

Chorus: La, la-la la la, (clap) la-la-
La, la-la la, la la-
La, la-la la la, (clap) la-la-
La, la-la, la la la.

**TRANSLITERATED HEBREW LYRICS:

Degel, degel, degel tov,
Degel tov sheli,
Bo tirkod, tirkod iti
B^e^Simchat Torah.

Chorus

**LYRICS IN HEBREW:

דֶּגֶל, דֶּגֶל, דֶּגֶל טוֹב,
דֶּגֶל טוֹב שֶׁלִּי,
בֹּא תִּרְקֹד, תִּרְקֹד אִתִּי,
בְּשִׂמְחַת תּוֹרָה.

פִּזְמוֹן:

לַ לַ-לַ לַ לַ (מְחִיאַת כַּף) לַ לַ
לַ לַ-לַ לַ לַ לַ...

TRANSLATION OF HEBREW:

Flag, flag, good flag
Good flag of mine
Come dance, dance with me
On Simchat Torah.
La, la-la, la, la, la, la...

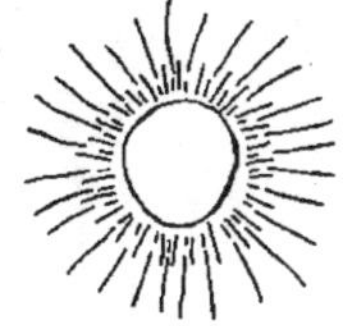

Here is a game to go with this song.

Have the children stand in a circle. Pick one child to go in the middle. As she goes round the inside of the circle, tapping each child on the head (as in "Duck, Duck Goose"), she sings (or everyone sings) in English or Hebrew until she gets to the last words 'Simchat Torah.' The last person she taps joins her in the middle of the circle and the two children hold hands and dance together as everyone else claps and sings the 'la-la-la' part of the song. Then the first tapper returns to the circle and the other child remains in the middle and repeats the process of walking around as she taps each child on the head. Play until all who want to be in the middle have had a turn.

Very sophisticated two-year-olds can play this with assistance, but three is the perfect age to introduce this game. As with any game where one goes in the middle, some of the children won't want to do so. See if you can get these children to go in the middle just for the dancing part, even if they won't be tappers.

Chanukah

חֲנוּכָּה

Holiday:

Chanukah (in very late November, or December)

What's it about?

A historical holiday. It commemorates the military and spiritual victory of the small army of rebels led by the Maccabee family against the ruling Seleucid (Syrian Greek) King Antiochus IV in 164 B.C.E., who tried to impose Greek religious beliefs and culture on the Jews in Palestine. It is a holiday about religious freedom and, in that sense, is related to Thanksgiving, whose original celebrants came to North America seeking religious freedom. The rabbis of the *Talmud* tell us that after the victory, when the Jews were cleaning and restoring the Temple in Jerusalem and preparing to rededicate it (the Temple had been desecrated by the Greek army), one night's worth of consecrated oil was found. Instead of lasting just one night, the oil burned for eight nights.

How is it celebrated?

The nine-branched Chanukah candelabra (called more correctly a *chanukiah* but referred to by Jews of Eastern European descent as a *menorah)* is lit in the window of the house so it can be seen by all who pass by. On the first night one candle is lit, and on each consecutive night one more candle is added. There are nine candles in the *chanukiah,* but the ninth, the *shamash* or servant candle, being used to light the others each night, is not counted. Its holder is higher, so that it stands slightly apart from the other candles. If you are facing the *chanukiah,* the candles are inserted from the right side to the left side (day one being on the far right, day two the next to farthest right, and so on). But they are lit from left to right, lighting the most recently added candle first. So we place the candles in Hebrew, but light them in English! This is another of the many symbols of Chanukah: Jews integrate the customs and cultures of the lands they live in to enrich, but never to abandon, their Jewish heritage.

Foods cooked in oil are eaten, such as potato pancakes (in Yiddish called *latkes)* or doughnuts (in Hebrew called *sufganiot).* There are parties and big meals; a betting game is played with a top called a *dreydl.** Chanukah songs are sung, and special prayers are said. Children are given presents (money, called Chanukah *gelt,* or toys); chocolate *'gelt'* is eaten, and the story of the Maccabees is told.

*Most books about Chanukah explain the *dreydl* game and the origins of the *dreydl* (Yiddish meaning 'spinning top').

Interdisciplinary ideas:

Literature:

One of the best Chanukah stories is Sholom Aleychem's "Benny's Luck," in *Holiday Tales of Sholom Aleychem,* selected and translated by Aliza Shervin.

Music:

Sing the *dreydl* song ("I had a little *dreydl...*") but substitute another substance for clay, such as: "I had a little *dreydl*/ I made it out of mud/ And when I tried to spin it/ It fell down with a thud!" A great way to liven up an old song even for older children, it is a favorite that could go on forever! Another Chanukah song loved by children from sophisticated three-year-olds up through middle school children, is "Nu in the Middle," by Leah Abrams. It is a riddle song and can be found in her collection of songs entitled *Apples on Holidays and Other Days* (see Music Resources).

Storytelling:

Have the children make up their own stories; either write down their ideas, or sit around in a circle and tell the stories to each other. Some story ideas: What do *dreydls* do in the middle of the night when we're asleep? What would happen if the *dreydl* wouldn't fall down? Talk with the children about what Chanukah was like when you were a child. Invite some grandparents to come to school to tell about their childhood Chanukahs and those of their parents and grandparents.

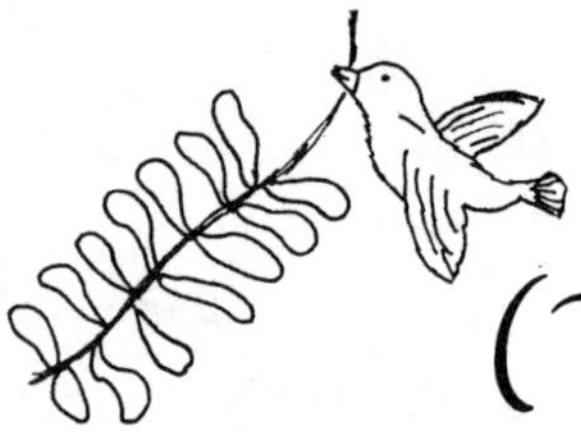

Drey Zich, Dreydele
(Turn Around, Little Dreydl)
דריי זיך דריידעלע

music by Avrom Goldfaden
Yiddish lyrics by Chane Mlotek, ACUM
English lyrics by Rachel Buchman
(Y.T.)

a waltz that gets faster and slower!

A7 A7

1. Turn a - round, turn a - round, Spin lit - tle drey - de - le,
3. Drey zich un drey zich un Drey zich, shoyn, drey - de - le,

Dm Dm

Turn a - round, turn a - round, Spin lit - tle drey - de - le,
Tants in a rin - ge - le, Tants in a rey - de - le,

A7 A7

One, two, three, one, two, three, Win, lit - tle drey - de - le,
Eynts, tsey, dray, eynts, tsvey, dray, Yin - ge - le, mey - de - le,

Dm Gm A7 Dm A7 Dm

Cha - nu - kah's here to - night, to - night!
Es iz shoyn Chan - u - kah do, shoyn do!

**1) Turn around, turn around,
Spin little dreydele,
Turn around, turn around,
Spin little dreydele,
One, two, three, one, two three,
Win little dreydele,
Chanukah's here tonight!

2) One, two, three, one, two, three,
Spin little dreydele,
One, two, three, one, two, three,
Win little dreydele,
One, two, three, one, two, three,
Turn around, dreydele,
Chanukah's here tonight!

3) Turn around, turn around,
Yingele, meydele,
Turn around, turn around,
My little dreydele,
Faster and faster and
Win little dreydele,
Chanukah's here tonight!

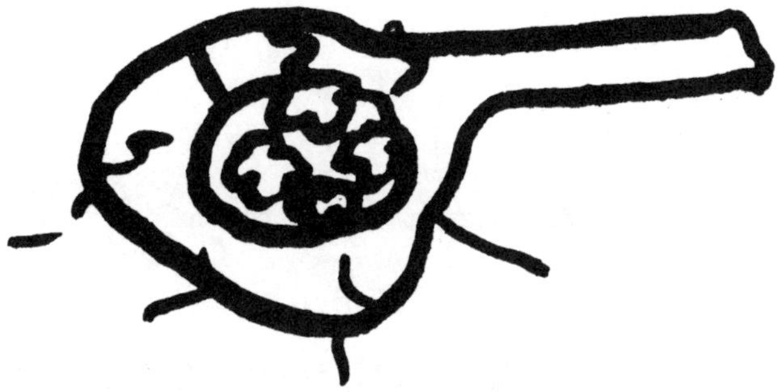

**TRANSLITERATED YIDDISH LYRICS:

Drey zich un drey zich un
Drey zich, shoyn, dreydele,
Tants in a ringele,
Tants in a reydele,
Eynts, tsvey, dray, eynts, tsvey, dray,
Yingele, meydele
Es iz shoyn Chanukah do, shoyn do!

Eynts, tsvey, dray, eynts, tsvey, dray,
Tants in a reydele
Eynts, tsvey, dray, eynts, tsvey, dray,
Yingele, meydele
Eynts, tsvey, dray, eynts, tsvey, dray,
Drey zich, shoyn, dreydele
Es iz shoyn Chanukah do, shoyn do!

**LYRICS IN YIDDISH:

דריי זיך און דריי זיך און
דריי זיך, שׁוין, דריידעלע
טאַנץ אין אַ רינגעלע,
טאַנץ אין אַ רעדעלע,
איינס, צוויי, דרייַ, איינס, צוויי, דרייַ,
יִינגעלע, מיידעלע
עס איז שׁוין חנוּכּה דאָ, שׁוין דאָ!

איינס, צוויי, דרייַ, איינס, צוויי, דרייַ,
טאַנץ אין אַ רעדעלע
איינס, צוויי, דרייַ, איינס, צוויי, דרייַ,
יִינגעלע, מיידעלע
איינס, צוויי, דרייַ, איינס, צוויי, דרייַ,
דריי זיך, שׁוין, דריידעלע
עס איז שׁוין חנוּכּה דאָ, שׁוין דאָ!

TRANSLATION OF YIDDISH LYRICS:

Turn yourself and turn yourself
And turn yourself, already, little dreydl,
Dance in a ring
Dance in a circle
One, two, three, one, two, three,
Little boy, little girl,
Chanukah is here already!

One, two, three, one, two, three,
Dance in a circle,
One, two, three, one, two, three,
Little boy, little girl,
One, two, three, one, two, three
Turn yourself around, already, little dreydl
Chanukah is here, already!

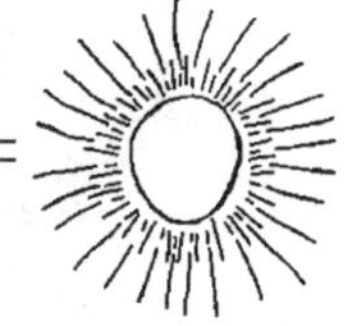

Here is a spinning game that goes with this song.

It is a listening game, too. Children ask to play it all year 'round.

Introduce the song and game like this (or make up something better): "During Chanukah, while children are asleep, *dreydls* wake up and play a spinning game. They taught me their game so I'll teach it to you. When the music plays fast, the *dreydls* spin fast, when the music plays slowly, the *dreydls* spin slowly, and when the music stops, what do you think happens?"

At this point, especially with young children who haven't had a lot of dreydl experience yet, we talk about the shape of the *dreydl* and the principle of motion they see illustrated by a top when it stops spinning. This would be a good time to bring in *dreydls* of different sizes and shapes and other tops to see how they spin.

I let the children make themselves look like *dreydls* in whatever way they like, but suggest they don't stand on one leg because they won't be able to spin very well.

When I sing the song, I vary the tempo without using a pattern - they pick up on a pattern too easily! When the children get very sensitive to the changes in tempo, I play tricks on them, stopping the song entirely in the middle of a verse ("Not a very good spin! Let's try it again!").

Sometimes the children won't fall down at all, despite the fact that they can barely remain standing. When they do this, we make up a story about faulty *dreydls*. We had to put them in a bag and take them back to the man at the *dreydl* shop (usually a crotchety old gent with an Eastern European accent). He tries the broken *dreydls* on his counter top, but they still don't work. When the man threatens to burn up all the bad *dreydls* either the children who won't fall down change their minds, or I, as owner of the *dreydls,* tell the man, "Never mind, I'll keep them anyway," and I put them back in my bag, take them home and that's the end of the story. Make up your own 'faulty *dreydl*' story.

I try to encourage the children to fall down when the music stops, though they'd rather play the broken *dreydl* game. They don't realize how much we adults learn about their listening skills and coordination from a game like this, so after they have played the joke of not falling one or two times, I insist they play the game correctly.

Happy chanukah

My Candles

traditional Chassidic melody
lyrics by Judith Kaplan Eisenstein
(S.W.S.)

slow and delicate
(sung in Bm on recording)

* Change the number with each verse until you have all eight candles. When you reach the eighth candle, sing, "I will set you, eight little candles,/ On this the last night of Chanukah."

In the window, where you can see the glow
From my menorah on newly fallen snow,
I will set you, one little candle,
On this the first night of Chanukah.

In the window, where you can see the glow
From my menorah on newly fallen snow,
I will set you, two little candles,
On this the second night of Chanukah.

(and so on until the eighth night)

In the window, where you can see the glow
From my menorah on newly fallen snow,
I will set you, eight little candles,
On this the last night of Chanukah.

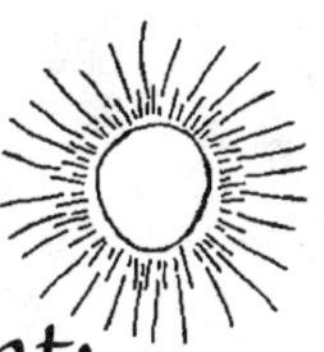  

Creative Movement:

With the youngest children:

Help them to make the candles of the *chanukiah* (Chanukah *menorah)* with their fingers. If they can't do that yet themselves, use pointer fingers to illustrate one and two; then count their fingers (as candles) for them, as in "This little piggy..." This song works well for children to listen to while resting or when they need something to quiet them down. When you get to the eighth night, have the children stand up to be the candles themselves. Have the children make a flame with their hands and arms over their heads (let each child illustrate this as they imagine it should be done). You can make believe you are lighting them. It adds a magical touch if you use a triangle or glockenspiel sounded over the head of each child to signify the lighting. Then, as you sing a verse on 'lay-lay-lay,' getting quieter and quieter, have the children slowly melt down to the ground until they are like the colored puddles of wax found on a *chanukiah.*

Talk about how candles grow *shorter* as they grow older (noting how this is just the opposite of what will happen to them as they get older!).

With older children, ages four and up:

Make a human *chanukiah* while singing the song. Pick one child to be the *shamash* (servant candle that is not counted). Have the rest of the children stand together as if in a box of candles. As you sing the song, have the *shamash* pick a child to be the first candle and place her at the far right of the space, as if you were facing the *chanukiah.* As you sing each night, have the *shamash* child add another child for each candle, until all eight candles stretch across the space from right to left. After singing the eighth night, have the *shamash* child 'light' all the other children, starting from left to right (so the last candle placed is the first one lit). The children make the flames over their heads with their hands and arms. Then, as you sing a verse on 'lay-lay-lay,' getting quieter and quieter, have the children slowly melt down to the ground until they are like the colored puddles of wax found on a *chanukiah.*

Tu biShvat

ט״ו בִּשְׁבָט

Holiday:

Tu biShvat (15th of Shvat, in January or early February)

What's it about?

An agricultural holiday, it is Jewish arbor day, the birthday of trees, a harbinger of spring. The trees were given a 'birthday' in the *Torah* because sacrifices and fruits that were eaten had to come from trees of a certain age. The only way to know the age of the trees was to establish a date as a birthday so that years could be reckoned from the planting of the tree at that date onwards. Today the holiday has taken on a much broader significance; we celebrate the 'birthday' of all trees, not just the ones we've planted, and recognize other plants as well.

How is it celebrated?

Trees are planted in the U.S. and Israel. It is traditional to have a feast, a Tu biShvat Seder, of the fruits of plants that are native to Israel.

Integrate these three trees – the green kind, family trees and the *Torah* (both the latter also ever growing). An important Hebrew phrase to learn and understand at this time of year is *Eyts Chaim* (Tree of Life), one of the most descriptive and poetic names for the *Torah.* What does it mean to love and care for the *Torah?* Just as no one can live without trees, no one can live without the *Torah,* a framework for an ethical life.

There are many references in the *Torah* to respect for nature, animals and plants. It is the perfect time of year to integrate environmental studies into a school curriculum or the family's activities.

Interdisciplinary ideas:

Literature:

"The Carrot Seed," by Ruth Krauss; "The Giving Tree," by Silverstein; "A Tree is Nice," by Udry.

Music:

There are many nice songs in English are about growing things, spring, planting; eg: "Early in the Morning," "The Green Grass Grew All Around," "Oats, Peas, Beans and Barley Grow." (Act out the song, including the actions of planting.) Talk about the foods that grow that children like to eat. Substitute their favorites for the oats, peas, beans, and barley, and 'plant' them while singing the song with the new suggestions. Bring in samples of oats, peas, beans, and barley, as well as the seeds of many of the fruits and vegetables they eat.

Social Studies:

Talk about trees the children know. Why should we take care of trees? Talk about the climate and geography of Israel - what does and doesn't grow there? Israeli produce includes oranges and other citrus fruits (a topic in itself), olives, figs, chickpeas, sunflower seeds, carob, avocadoes, sesame – not the Street! Bring in some of the more exotic fruits for them to taste. Just as deliciously grown in Israel are tomatoes, strawberries, and cucumbers. Compare the sizes and shapes of the seeds, pods and pits of these plants. Point out that plants come in a variety of shapes, sizes and colors, just like people do.

Science Project:

Plant a tree at your school. Tend it with the children. Plant parsley in class which can be used for your Pesach *Seder.*

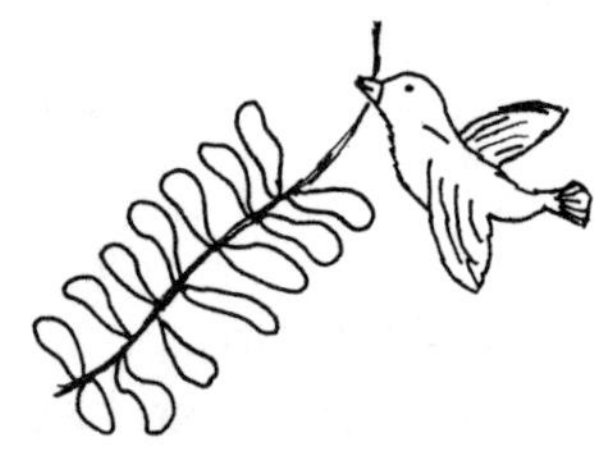

Tu-Tu-Tu-Tu, on Tu biShvat

(originally titled: Kach Holchim haShotlim / Here Come the Planters)

כַּךְ הוֹלְכִים הַשּׁוֹתְלִים

music by J. Admon (Gorochov)
Hebrew lyrics by Y. Sheinberg, ACUM
English lyrics by Rachel Buchman,
except for first line of each verse by
Judith Eisenstein Kaplan
(S.C.)

a brisk, walking tempo, with pride

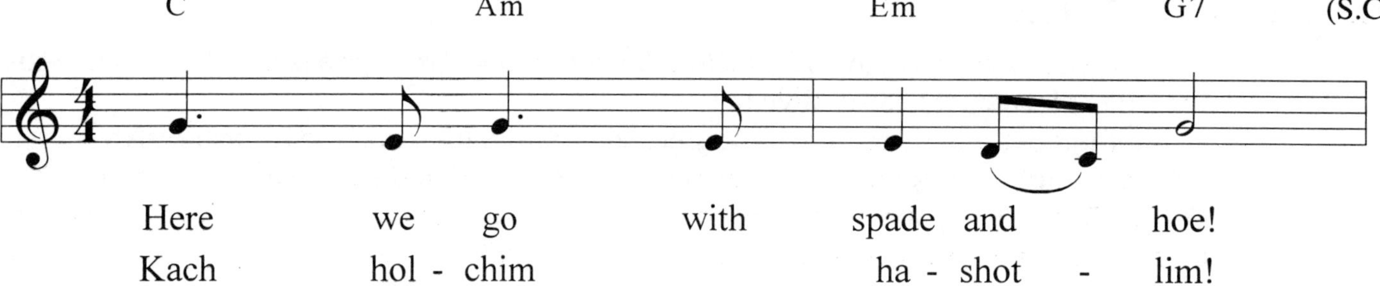

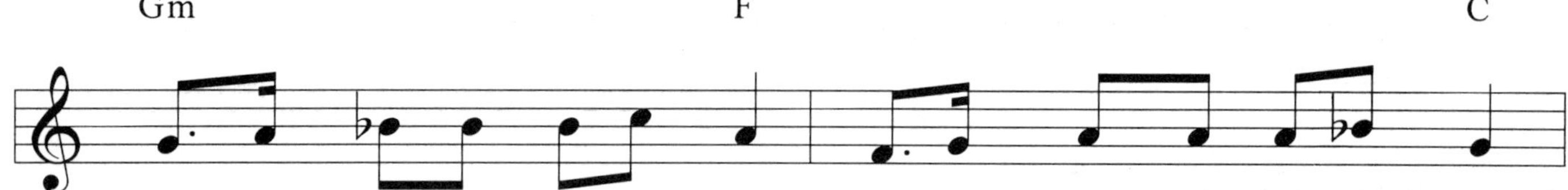

**1) Here we go with spade and hoe!
From the city and the town
Everyone come gather 'round,
Come and plant a tree with me

Chorus: On Tu-Tu-Tu-Tu, on Tu biShvat
On Tu-Tu-Tu-Tu, on Tu biShvat.

2) Here we go with spade and hoe!
Everybody dig, dig, dig,
Make the hole so big, big, big,
This is how we plant a tree
Chorus

3) Here we go with spade and hoe!
Little tree go in the ground,
Pat the dirt now, all around,
This is how we plant a tree
Chorus

4) Here we go with spade and hoe!
Give some water to your tree,
Rain come down and please help me,
This is how we plant a tree
Chorus

5) Here we go with spade and hoe!
Sun come out and shine each day,
My tree will grow and I will play,
This is how we plant a tree
Chorus

6) Here we go with spade and hoe!
Happy birthday, little tree!
Next year you'll be big as me,
I can hardly wait to see
Next Tu-Tu-Tu-Tu, next Tu biShvat
On Tu-Tu-Tu-Tu, on Tu biShvat.

Creative Movement/Science Activities:

Have the children start by shouldering their gardening tools. Introduce new vocabulary, such as spade, hoe, rake, wheelbarrow; bring in as many of the items as possible so they can see what they really are and how they are used in a garden. Walk around as if walking to the tree-planting place; or take a short trip up and down the hall or outdoors, singing the Tu-Tu-Tu part of the song.

As you sing through the verses, see if the children can tell you what the plants need to grow (soil, water, sunlight) *before* you sing it in the verse. Have them make believe they are doing what they are singing about. Let the children decide how to act out the sun and the rain, etc.

When you get to the verse, 'happy birthday, little tree,' have the children get down to their tree's level and wish the tree a happy birthday. Talk to the children about the fact that plants need our care and attention, that they are living things.

Be sure the children sing along with the chorus. After a while they will sing along throughout the song.

After singing the second-to-last verse, have the children make believe they are seeds underground or baby trees. Then sing them a verse on 'la-la-la,' as they slowly grow, stretching up their branches and leaves. Be sure you talk to the children about how slowly trees grow, much slower than people, and how long they live.

Look at clear photos or drawings of different types of trees. Teach the children the names and distinguishing features of the trees in your area. Have them collect bark and leaves and make a tree collage or portrait.

Do an experiment with several plants, all of the same kind and size. Your control plant will have proper light, soil, and water. Raise plant number one in a closet or dark place, but give it soil and water. Raise number two in a sunny place with soil, but don't give it water. Raise number three in a sunny place with water, but don't give it soil. Try different sets of variables. See what happens. Make sure the children check the plants regularly and talk about what changes they observe.

TRANSLATION OF HEBREW LYRICS:
(The second and third verses are not commonly sung any longer.)

So come the planters,
A song in their hearts and spades in hand,
From the city and the village,
From the valley, from the mountain

chorus:
On Tu-Tu-Tu-Tu, on Tu biShvat,
On Tu-Tu-Tu-Tu, on Tu biShvat.

Why do you planters come?
We will strike the soil and the rock
And we will dig holes all around,
On the mountains and the plains,
On Tu-Tu-Tu-Tu, on Tu biShvat...

What will be here, planters?
Seedlings will come up in all the holes,
A virgin forest will spread its shade
Over our melancholy land,
On Tu-Tu-Tu-Tu, on Tu biShvat...

**ORIGINAL HEBREW LYRICS:
(by Sheinberg; not a translation of the English lyrics on p. 51. Written before the establishment of the State of Israel)

כַּךְ הוֹלְכִים הַשּׁוֹתְלִים
רֹן בַּלֵּב וְאֵת בַּיָּד
מִן הָעִיר וּמִן הַכְּפָר
מִן הָעֵמֶק , מִן הָהָר,

פִּזְמוֹן:
בְּט"וּ - ט"וּ - ט"וּ - ט"וּ , בְּט"וּ בִּשְׁבָט
בְּט"וּ - ט"וּ - ט"וּ - ט"וּ , בְּט"וּ בִּשְׁבָט

לָמָּה בָּאתֶם הַשּׁוֹתְלִים?
נַךְ בַּקַּרְקַע וּבַצֹּר
וְגוּמוֹת סָבִיב נַחְפֹּר
בֶּהָרִים וּבַמִּישׁוֹר,
בְּט"וּ - ט"וּ - ט"וּ - ט"וּ...

מַה יְּהֵא פֹּה הַשּׁוֹתְלִים?
שָׁתִיל יָבוֹא בְּכָל גּוּמָה
יַעַר עַד יִפְרֹשׂ צִלּוֹ
עַל אַרְצֵנוּ עֲגוּמָה,
בְּט"וּ - ט"וּ - ט"וּ - ט"וּ...

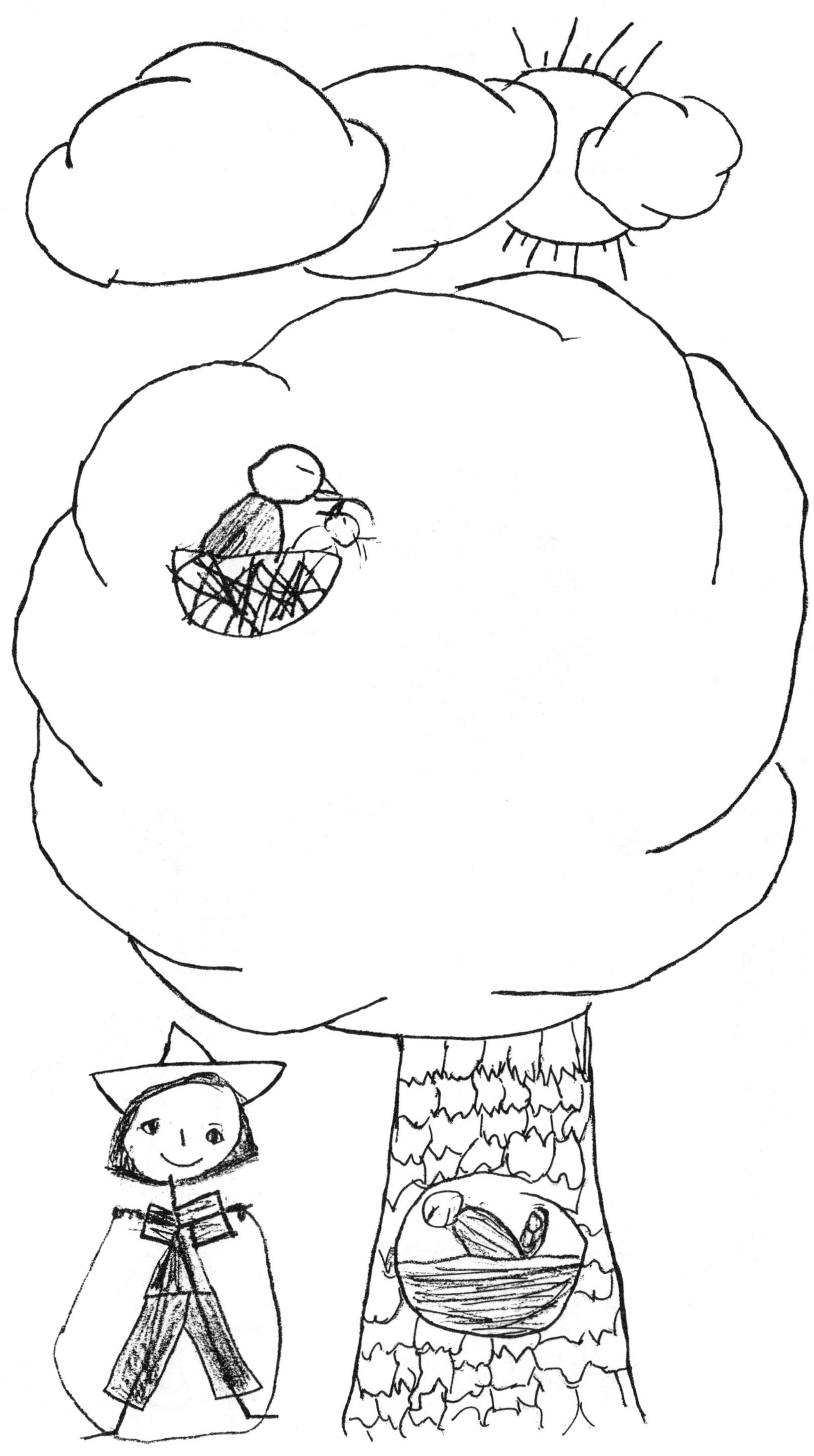

Purim

פּוּרִים

Holiday:

Purim (Feast of Lots, in late February or March)

What's it about?

A historical holiday. The story is told in the Book of Esther that Haman, advisor to King Ahashverosh of Babylonia, plotted to have all the Jews of the land destroyed. The plot was discovered and foiled by the Jewish Queen Esther and her uncle, Mordecai. Haman and his evil sons and ministers are then executed by order of the king. The heroine of the story is Esther the Queen. The story is told in classic form, each scene contrasting greatly in feeling, as it builds up to an intense, dramatic climax and resolution.

How is it celebrated?

To celebrate Purim properly one must hear the story of Esther read aloud, give gifts to the needy, send gifts of food to friends and relatives, and eat a festive meal.* On the evening Purim begins and on the following morning, the Book of Esther is read aloud in synagogue from a scroll. Every time Haman's name is read, the congregation drowns out the reader by shaking noisy shakers and other noise makers called *groggers* (in Yiddish) or *ra'ashanim* (in Hebrew). Everyone dresses in costumes, there are parties, special songs are sung, and stuffed triangle shaped cookies are eaten. They are called *homentashn* (Yiddish for 'Haman pockets') or *ozney-Haman* (Hebrew for 'ears of Haman'). Farcical plays tell the story of Purim. Gifts of *homentashn*, sweets and fruits are exchanged with friends. It is traditional to donate money, time, or something else to charity on this holiday. It is a Mardi Gras-type festival with a serious and, unfortunately, still relevant message. It is said that one should drink so much in celebration of Haman's demise that one cannot tell the difference between wicked Haman and brave Mordecai.

A theme that is relevant to Purim, which can be discussed age-appropriately with all children, is that of taking responsibility for oneself, and by taking responsibility, taking action. This theme is best expressed by Rabbi Hillel (c. 50 B. C. E. - 25 C. E.). He said, "If I am not for myself, who will be for me? If I am only for myself, what am I? And if not now, when?"

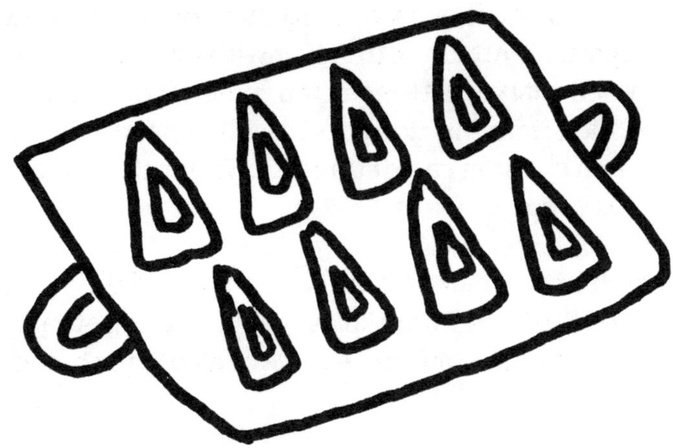

*The Hebrew names for these three *mitzvot* (commandments) are, respectively: *matanot ha-evyonim, mishlo-ach manot* (*shalach manos* in Yiddish, as you'll see in the song that follows) and *se-udat Purim.*

Art:

Purim Groggers (noise makers)

Can be made out of empty coffee cans or frozen juice cans. Fill them with a handful of beans or rice; secure the tops with tape; cover with colored paper or wrapping paper, decorate with markers or paint.

Wooden Spoon Puppets

Let the children draw faces on the spoons with markers. Glue on cotton or yarn hair. Add color to the cotton hair with water-based markers. Make crowns of foil. Glue felt hands to the stick part of spoon or make a felt costume and glue it to the upper part of the stick so the child can easily hold onto the stick handle. You can also attach the costume by looping a rubberband round and round the cloth at the neck of the puppet. Leave a bit of cloth sticking out. When the rubber band is sufficiently tight, fold the extra bit of cloth down to cover the rubberband.

Larger than Life Puppets

Take 1/2 gallon plastic milk or juice jugs (cleaned and dried). With indelible markers draw a face, or cut out features from material and glue them on. Make the face on the side of the jug opposite from the handle, using the corner as the nose. Then attach yarn skeins of hair using masking tape and glue. Tie scarves on or put on a hat.

Before attaching the head to a broomstick handle, drape large pieces of fabric over the top of the handle, letting them hang naturally all around (the broomstick should be in the middle of the cloth piece). If you like, you can 'belt' the material a foot or two down to give the puppet a 'waist.' Add necklaces or other accessories and then fix the jug head on top securely.

You can use elbow length gloves sewn onto the sides of the cloth as arms and hands. Tack the glove on so you can insert your own hand or a short stick to manipulate the glove. This makes operating the puppet more complicated, but you'll have a more expressive puppet. However, with or without the moving arm, these huge puppets are great fun for children.

Small Puppets

Use a barbecue skewer stuck into a wine bottle cork. Draw the face of the puppet on the cork with indelible marker, using fabric store wiggly or google eyes (white with moving black pupils; they come in many sizes). Attach cotton hair with glue to the tops of the corks. Add color to the hair with water based markers. Using scrap material or felt, cut out a body, adding hands of a contrasting color. Decorate the cloth bodies with sparkles and little bells. These little puppets are good to use when children can sit up close. The cork puppets are delicate and should not be handled by the children.

In Coopersmith's *The Songs We Sing* you can find all the verses to the song, "Wicked, Wicked Man." The verses tell the basic Purim story. Let your puppets act it out. Each time you get to the chorus, "Oh, today we'll merry, merry be...," have all of the characters 'sing' and 'dance' together.

Woodenspoon Puppets

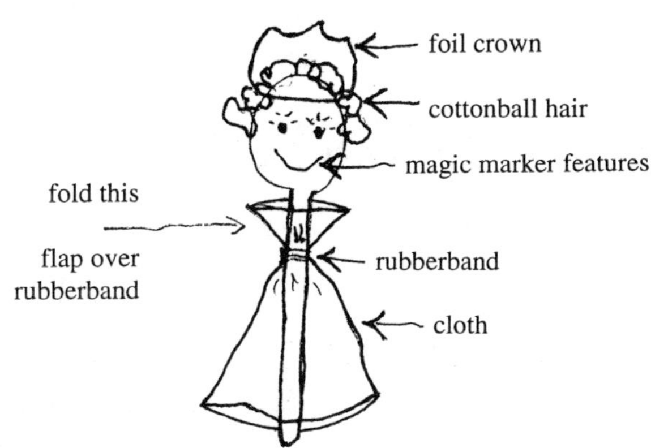

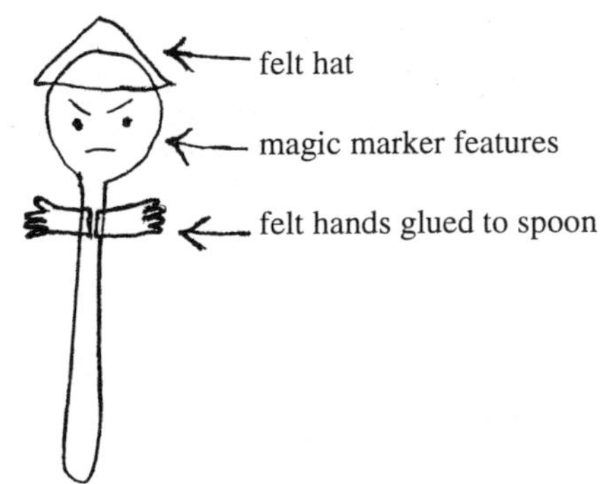

Milk Jug Puppets

1) Create head

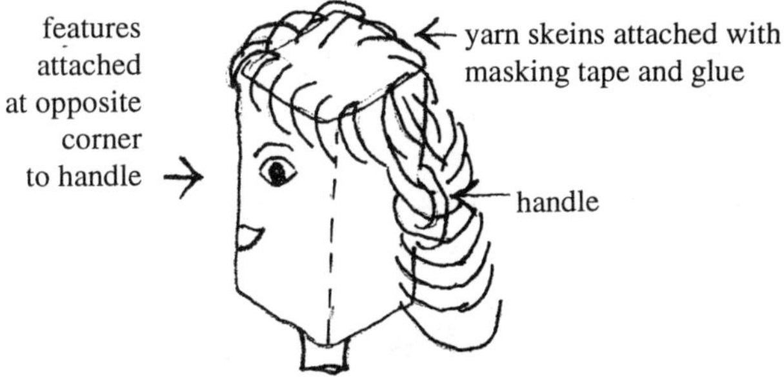

2) Drape one or two pieces of cloth over broomstick *before* attaching jug head.

3) Decorate "clothes"

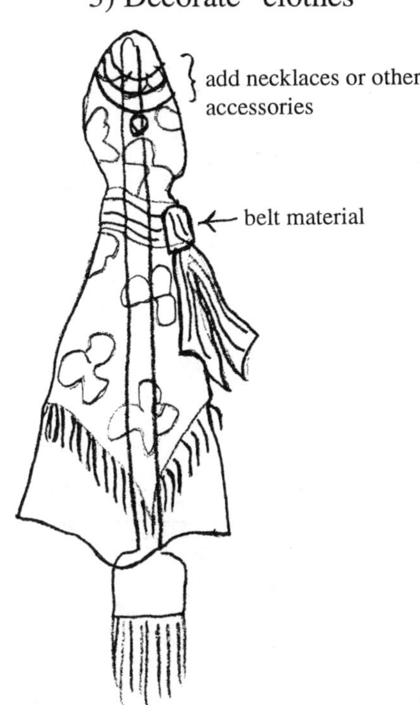

4) attach jughead to broomstick - add extra material to top of handle if jug doesn't stay on securely

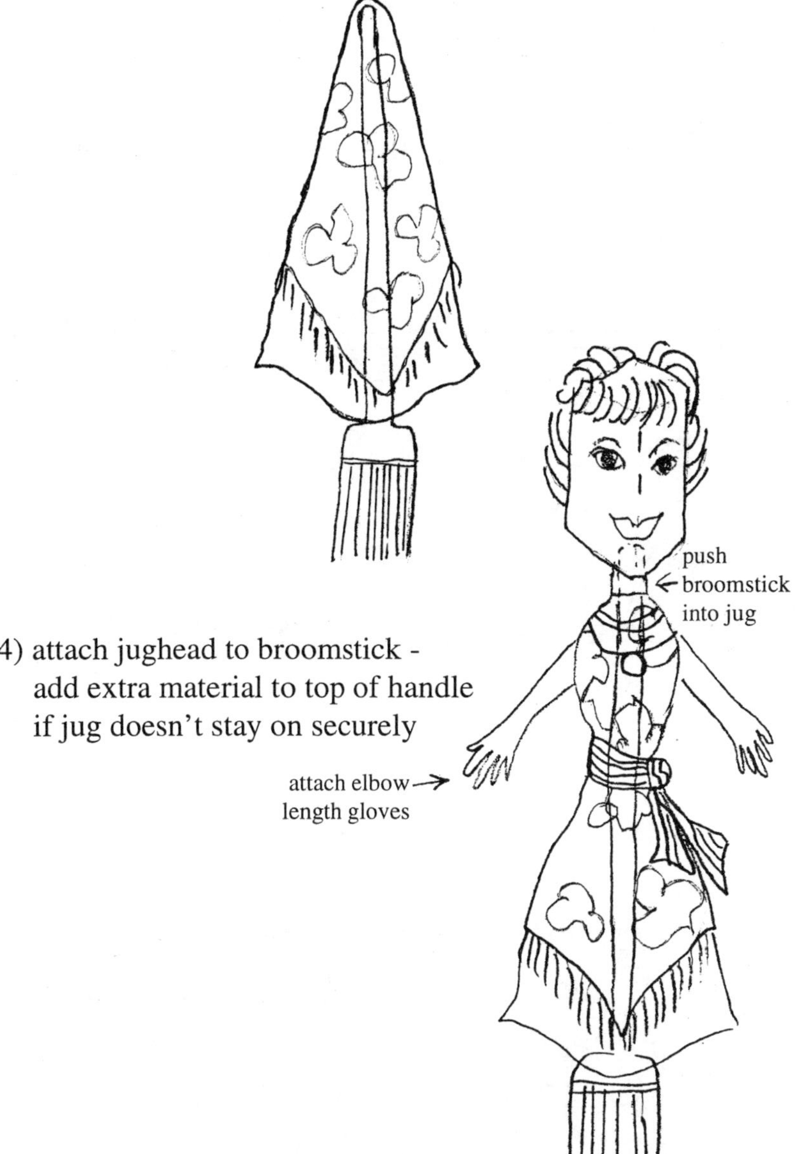

Rash Ra-ashan! (Rrrssh, Purim Shakers)

רַשׁ רַעֲשָׁן

and Purim haYom (Purim is Today)

פּוּרִים הַיּוֹם

**TRANSLITERATION OF HEBREW LYRICS:

Rash ra-ashan,
say: Shake your shakers! (groggers! ra-ashanim!)
Rash ra-ashan
say: Shake your shakers! (groggers! ra-ashanim!)
B^{e}chag Purim, b^{e}chag Purim!
(repeat verse)

Purim, Purim, Purim hayom
Chag Purim hayom!
Purim, Purim, Purim hayom
Chag Purim hayom!

**LYRICS IN HEBREW:

רַשׁ רַעֲשָׁן! רַשׁ רַעֲשָׁן!
רַשׁ רַעֲשָׁן! רַשׁ רַעֲשָׁן!
בְּחַג פּוּרִים, בְּחַג פּוּרִים.

פּוּרִים, פּוּרִים, פּוּרִים הַיּוֹם,
חַג פּוּרִים הַיּוֹם.
פּוּרִים, פּוּרִים, פּוּרִים הַיּוֹם
חַג פּוּרִים הַיּוֹם.

Musical Activities:

Talk with the children about listening to contrasts in music, and in the sounds they hear around them on the street, in the school yard, at the beach, and so on. There are loud sounds, quiet sounds, fast and slow sounds. When singing this song, sing the first two lines ("Rash ra-ashan/Rash ra-ashan") very quietly. In between the lines of singing, play a percussion instrument, guitar, or piano very loudly. In the second half of the song ("Purim, Purim, Purim today, Purim is today," etc.) play your instrument loudly the whole time. Give the children percussion instruments to play, or let them use their homemade *groggers* (Purim noisemakers). After two or three repetitions children even as young as eighteen months will get the idea. They delight in the contrast and so manage to control their instruments for the very quiet part before the torrent of sound breaks loose. The only time they have trouble controlling their instruments is on the first day when the instruments are distributed. When they become proficient at holding their instruments quietly during the quiet singing, see if they can learn to *play* their instruments quietly during the quiet section. Bursting into the loud, second section will be even more fun.

This is an excellent song for developing listening skills, group dynamics, coordination between what they hear and what they do, and sensitivity to their own actions. And it is great practice for blotting out Haman's name at the *Megillah* reading. *(Megillah* is the Hebrew word for scroll. Have you heard the expression from Yiddish - "She told me the whole *megillah"?* It means "she told me the whole, long story," but it literally means "the whole scroll!").

With older children you can also explore what happens to the sounds of instruments when they are shaken, scraped, struck, or blown harder or faster, as opposed to slower or more gently.

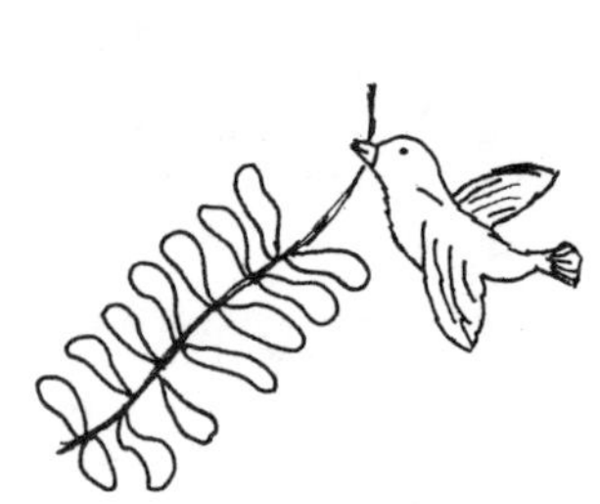

Hop! Mayne Homentashn
(Hey! My Homentashen)

האָפּ! מײַנע המן-טאַשן

Yiddish folk song
English lyrics by Rachel Buchman
Happy Valley Music, BMI
(T.J.F.)

lively and in jest

C G C
Yach - ne went to mar - ket, She
There's sometimes rain and sometimes snow

G C
brings her sack a - long, She's
Drip - ping from the roof - tops,

G C G7
off to buy some flour and she hums a Pu - rim
Yach-ne's sack of flour splits o - pen with a

C F
song. Chorus: Hop! May - ne ho - men - ta - shn!
pop!

G C G
Hop! May - ne vay - se Hop! Mit may - ne

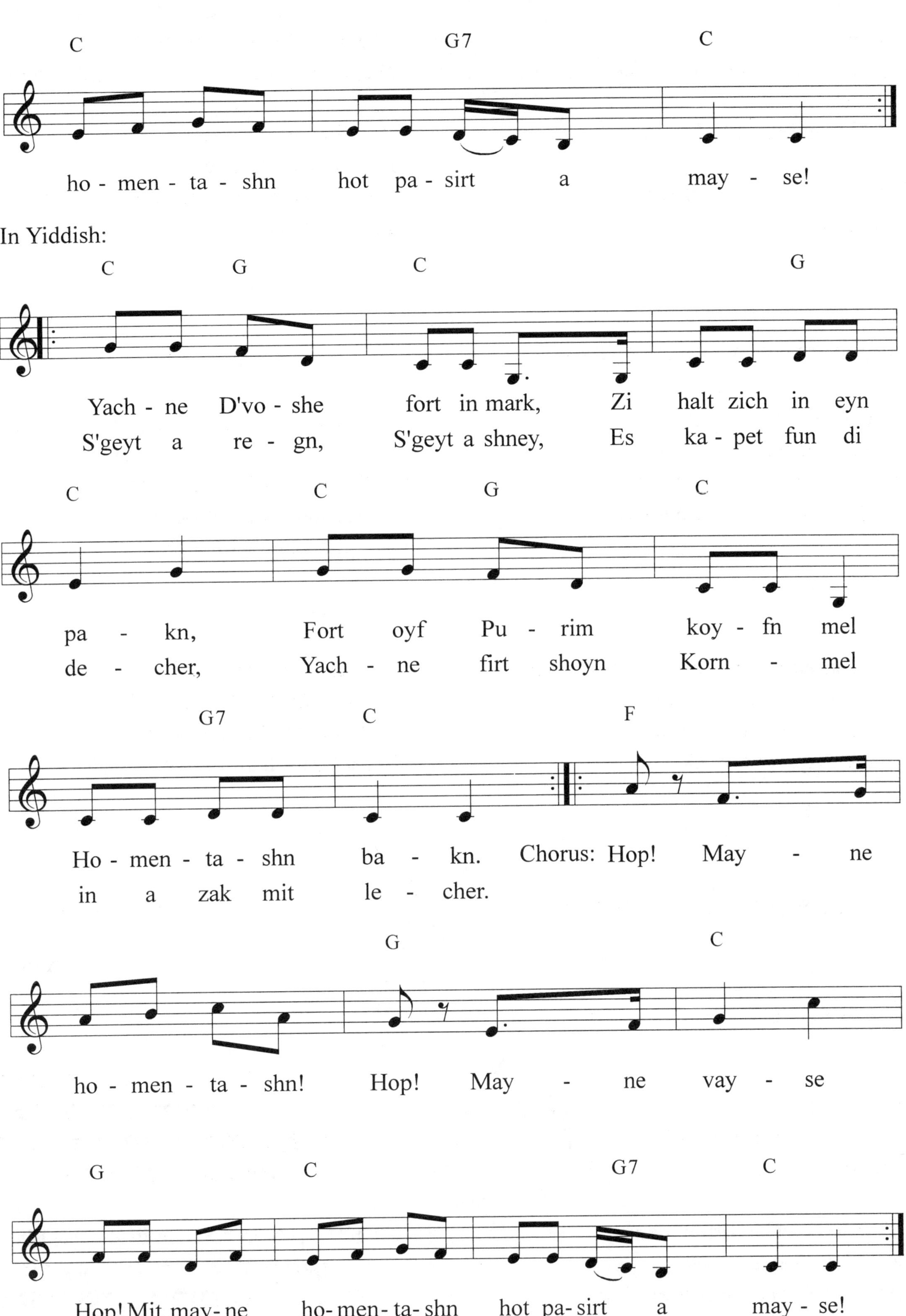
C G7 C
ho - men - ta - shn hot pa - sirt a may - se!
In Yiddish:
C G C G
Yach - ne D'vo - she fort in mark, Zi halt zich in eyn
S'geyt a re - gn, S'geyt a shney, Es ka - pet fun di
C C G C
pa - kn, Fort oyf Pu - rim koy - fn mel
de - cher, Yach - ne firt shoyn Korn - mel
G7 C F
Ho - men - ta - shn ba - kn. Chorus: Hop! May - ne
in a zak mit le - cher.
G C
ho - men - ta - shn! Hop! May - ne vay - se
G C G7 C
Hop! Mit may - ne ho - men - ta - shn hot pa - sirt a may - se!

**Chorus:
(sung between each verse or between every other verse)

Hop! Mayne homentashn!
Hop! Mayne vayse
Hop! Mit mayne homentashn
Hot pasirt a mayse!

TRANSLATION OF CHORUS:
(but sing it in Yiddish; it sounds much better!)

Hey! My homentashen
Hey! My white one
Hey! Something happened
To my homentashen!

**TRANSLATION OF YIDDISH LYRICS:

1) Yachne walks to market,
She brings her sack along,
She's off to buy some flour
And she hums a Purim song.

2) There's sometimes rain, there's some-times snow
Dripping from the rooftops,
Yachne's sack of flour
Splits open with a pop!

Chorus

3) She forgets the honey, forgets the eggs,
She even forgets the yeast,
She bakes her homentashen
In the oven for a week.

4) Yachne brings her shalach-mones
To Yente, her best friend...
A couple of homentashen,
Half raw, half burned!

Chorus

**TRANSLITERATION OF YIDDISH LYRICS:

Chorus:
(sung between each verse
or between every other verse)

Hop! Mayne homentashn!
Hop! Mayne vayse
Hop! Mit mayne homentashn
Hot pasirt a mayse!

1) Yachne Dvoshe fort in mark,
Zi halt zich in eyn pakn,
Fort oyf Purim koyfn mel
Homentashn bakn.

**LYRICS IN YIDDISH:

צוזינג:

האָפּ! מײַנע המן-טאַשן!
האָפּ! מײַנע ווײַסע
האָפּ! מיט מײַנע המן-טאַשן
האָט פּאַסירט אַ מעשׂה!

יאַכנע-דוואָשע פֿאָרט אין מאַרק,
זי האַלט זיך אין איין פּאַקן,
פֿאָרט אויף פּורים קויפֿן מעל
המן-טאַשן באַקן.

2) S'geyt a regn, s'geyt a shney, Es kapet fun di decher, Yachne firt shoyn kornmel In a zak mit lecher.	ס׳גייט אַ רעגן, ס׳גייט אַ שניי, ס׳קאַפּעט פון די דעכער, יאַכנע פירט שוין קורנמעל אין אַ זאַק מיט לעכער!
Chorus	צוזינג
3) Nit kayn honig, nit kayn mohn Un fargesn heyvn, Yachne macht shoyn homentashn, Es bakt zich shoyn in oyvn.	ניט קײַן הוניג, ניט קײַן מאָן און פאַרגעסן הייוון, יאַכנע מאַכט שוין המן-טאַשן, ס׳באַקט זיך שוין אין אויוון.
Yachne trogt shoyn shalach-mones Tsu der bobe Yente - Tsvey-dray homentashn, Halb roy, halb farbrente!	יאַכנע טראָגט שוין שלח-מנות צו דער באָבע יענטע - צײ-דרײַ המן-טאַשן, האַלב רוי, האַלב פאַרברענטע!
Chorus	צוזינג

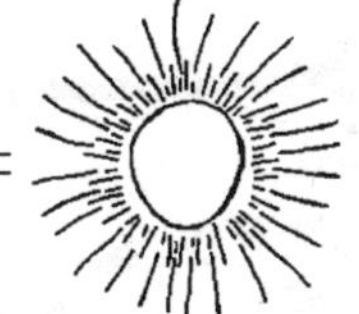

Creative Movement:

The name 'Yachne Dvoshe' is pejorative. A Yachne is a *yente,* a gossip. The two names together suggest an old hag, someone who always has bad luck, or for whom things always turn out poorly. She is a stock character.

Whether children understand Yiddish or hear it in translation, they always appreciate the rough humor of this song. They love acting out the story of incompetent Yachne Dvoshe. For the singing of the chorus ask the children to make themselves into the triangle shape of a *homentashn* and to hop up and down. Let them figure out their own way of depicting themselves as giant *homentashn.* Have them start the first verse by putting a make believe sack over their shoulders and trudging off to market to buy flour. When you get to the line 'splits open with a pop!', have the children make a popping sound with their mouths. Be sure younger children realize Yachne spilled her flour. Imagine a grown-up spilling! Then let them mime mixing batter and putting the cookies in the oven, giving each other *shalach manot* (gifts of delicious things to eat for Purim), only to find that half the *homentashn* are burnt (explain to young ones what this means) and the other half are raw! (Explain this word, too.) Kids love to make faces when they 'taste' the terrible cookies!

Pesach

פֶּסַח

Holiday:

Pesach (Passover, in late March or April)

What's it about?

A historical, agricultural, and philosophical holiday, it commemorates the exodus of the Israelites from Egypt, and celebrates freedom from slavery. Next to the High Holy Days (Rosh haShanah and Yom Kippur) it is the most important holiday of the Jewish calendar; for many it *is* the most important. Pesach, too, is a kind of new year, a celebration of spring and a new life in freedom. Children can understand the story and the significance of this holiday, and they have a lot to do with its celebration.

How it's celebrated:

An elaborate feast, called a *Seder,* is prepared during which all the participants read the story of the exodus from Egypt while performing certain symbolic rituals at the table. The story is contained in a standardized text called the *Haggadah* (literally 'the narration'). The *Haggadah* tells the exodus story, but it is also a manual for conducting the *Seder.* It includes a guide to the rituals performed during the *Seder,* selections from the *Torah,* rabbinic commentary on those selections, prayers, Passover *z'mirot* (hymns). Children are responsible for several rituals during the *Seder* and are an essential part of it.

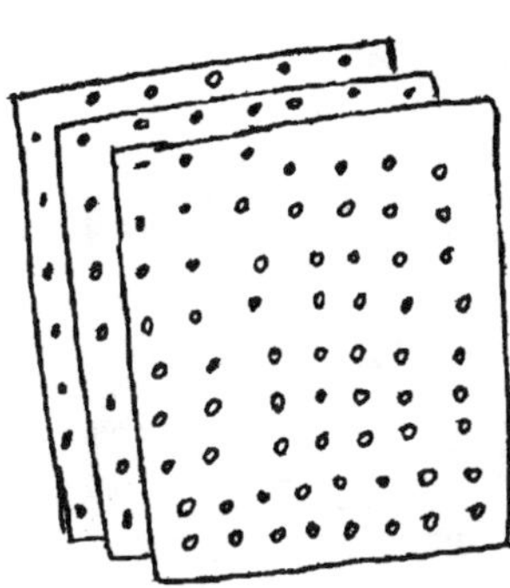

The holiday lasts seven or eight days,* during which time the eating of leavened bread and many other foods is forbidden. *Matzah* (flat crackers made of specially grown and prepared flour mixed with water) is eaten instead of bread, pasta, cake, and other foods made of grains. Instead dishes are created with *matzah* meal or potatoes. Sephardic Jews (originally from Spain, now mainly from the Middle East) traditionally eat rice and beans during Pesach while Ashkenazic Jews (from central, eastern, and northern Europe) do not. The *Haggadah* we use today closely corresponds to one in use in the 11th Century, but the earliest parts of it are as old as the First and Second centuries C.E.

*The length of the holiday depends on whether one lives in Israel or what type of Jewish congregation one belongs to in the U.S.

Interdisciplinary ideas:

Literature:

Sholom Aleychem's "A Ruined Passover" and "The Passover Exiles" from *Holiday Tales* of Sholom Aleychem, edited and translated by Aliza Shevrin are a delight for adults as well as children. These are sophisticated and ironic stories suitable for younger children if long descriptive passages and asides are skipped or summarized. For older children these stories are a history lesson about life in the European *shetl* with a twist. Explanations will be necessary for most children, but well worth the effort. A few other books: *The Carp in the Bathtub* by Barbara Cohen, *The Matzah That Papa Brought Home* by Fran Manushkin, and *The Passover Parrot* by Evelyn Zusman. An entertaining way for young children to find out how *matzah* is made is to read *The Mouse in the Matzah Factory* by Francine Medoff. Reading from the beginning of Exodus to Exodus 25. 27 is the best introduction to the Passover story since the actual story is not fully or clearly told in the *Haggadah.*

Social Studies:

Take children to a museum to see Egyptian relics. Show them photos of the Pyramids, the Sphyinx, the Nile. Tell them how they could actually go to Eygpt and see the land where Moses grew up, and lived, and the desert he crossed. Young children love a short museum trip when they know what to look for!

Take a trip to a Passover *matzah* bakery. The local Jewish Community Center often sets one up before Passover or they will know where you can find such a bakery in your area.

Make a Matzah

by Hyman Reznick
2nd verse by Rachel Buchman
(from Ben Aronin's "Jolly Jingles")

a walking tempo

G D

D G

  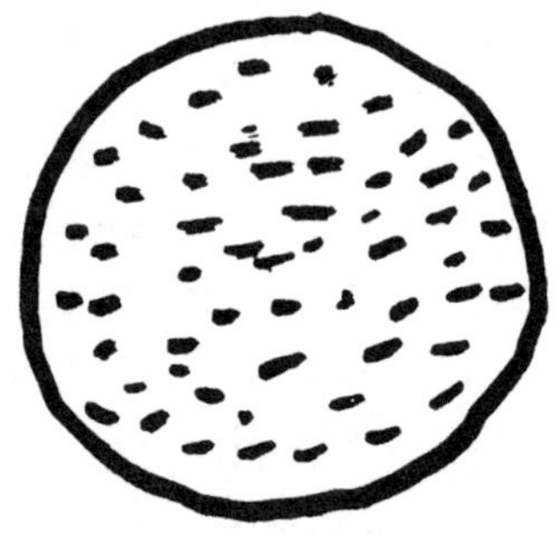

1) Make a matzah, pat! pat! pat!
clap each time you say 'pat'
Do not make it fat! fat! fat!
gesture round and fat
Make a matza, flat! flat! flat!
brush hands together each time you say 'flat'
Make a matza, just like that!
snap

2) First you pat it
clap hands
Then you flat it
brush hands together
Put it in the oven* very hot...
gesture sliding into the oven
Pull it out quick!
gesture pulling out the matzas quickly as you say
Whoosh! What have you got?

(repeat first verse)

Then you eat it!

*As one child suggested to me, everyone should put on their oven mitts before we put the *matzah* in the oven! Talk about cooking safety. Kids are very aware of and serious about safety precautions and enjoy practicing them.

Have the children tell you what they would like to put on their *matzah.* All of you make believe you are spreading and loading the stuff on. Usually you end up with a huge 'pile' of toppings! Then make believe you are eating it. Try to make *matzah*-like flat breads using a non-rising dough recipe and rolling the dough out as thin as possible.

Where is Baby Moses?

by Jackie Weissman Silberg
Miss Jackie Publishing, BMI
additional lyrics by Rachel Buchman

in a medium, rocking tempo
(sung an octave lower on recording)

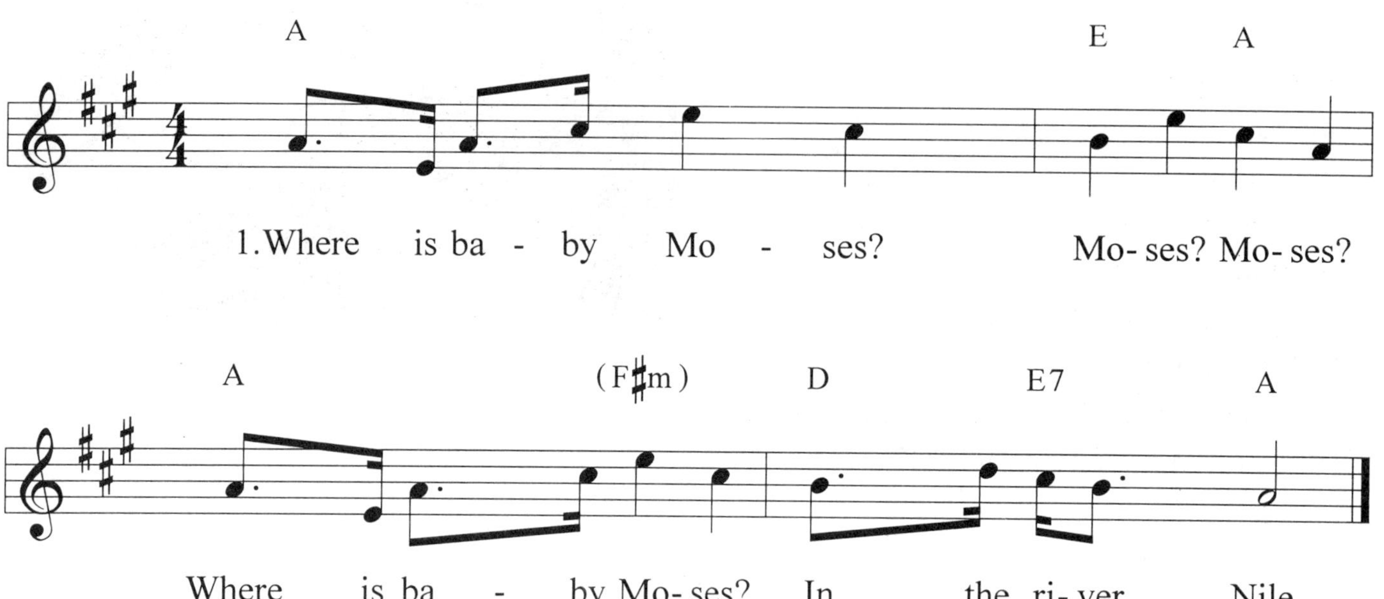

(All the gestures should be done rhythmically to the music and repeated throughout the verse until the last line about the Nile.)

1) Where is baby Moses?
shade eyes from the sun, turning head this way and that as if looking
Moses? Moses?
Where is baby Moses?
In the river Nile.
make wavy motions with the hands moving from left to right at about waist level

2) He's floating in a basket,
shape a basket with both arms, rocking it in front of you
Basket, basket.
He's floating in a basket
In the river Nile.
make wavy motions with the hands moving from left to right at about waist level

3) The princess she is swimming*
leisurely swimming motions
Swimming, swimming.
The princess she is swimming
In the river Nile.
make wavy motions with the hands moving from left to right at about waist level

4) She finds the baby Moses,
gently lift up the baby out of the basket and cradle it
Moses, Moses.
She finds the baby Moses
In the river Nile.
make wavy motions with the hands moving from left to right at about waist level

5) She takes him to the palace,

raise hands above the head to make a pyramid-like shape

Palace, palace.

She takes him to the palace

By the river Nile.

make wavy motions with the hands moving from left to right at about waist level

6) And there our Moses grows up

stretch up, starting at the floor and reaching up to the sky

Grows up, grows up.

And there our Moses grows up

By the river Nile.

make wavy motions with the hands moving from left to right at about waist level

*In the *Torah* the story tells that the daughter of Pharaoh came to the river to bathe. It is easy to imagine that as the princess was washing she also took some time to enjoy the water. Children are much more attracted to the image of the Princess swimming than bathing!

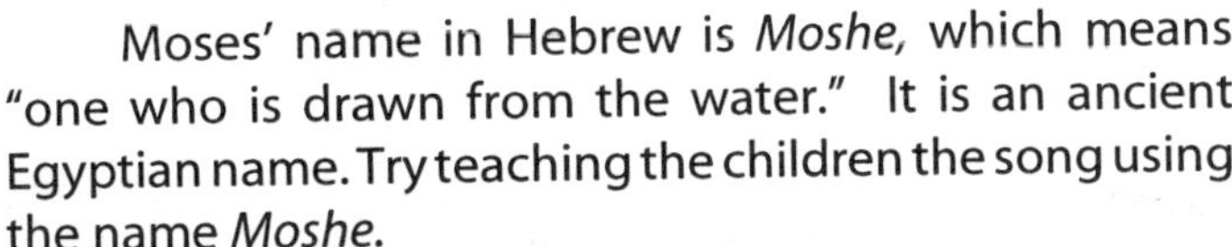

Moses' name in Hebrew is *Moshe,* which means "one who is drawn from the water." It is an ancient Egyptian name. Try teaching the children the song using the name *Moshe.*

This song is rich in its potential to teach children about the world of the Passover story. When teaching the song, take the time to illustrate with words, and with pictures if you have them, the details of life on the Nile. Each verse offers a different focus.

The first verse introduces the dire situation of the Hebrew slaves (Moses' mother had to hide him). Tell them that when Moses' mother put him into the bulrushes, his sister was watching to see what would happen. You can talk about how cruel the Pharaoh was at the time of Moses (as opposed to the Pharaoh at the time of Joseph, for example). You can talk about the sunny, hot weather in Egypt, which is why you must shade your eyes to look for the baby. Find Egypt on a map.

For the second verse talk about rivers. Unless they live near a river that affects their lives, most young children don't know what a river is. Talk about the teeming life that surrounds rivers. Learn the names and locations of other great rivers in the world. Find out what the bank of the river was like. Purchase bulrushes at a florist and bring them in for the children to see. Construct a tar-lined basket for a baby doll (you can use glue or another waterproof substance) and then try to float it.

The third verse involves the princess. Talk about how people bathed in rivers, washed their clothes there, and so on. (Don't forget about the crocodiles in the Nile!) Tell them how the princess had lovely soaps and perfumes to wash with. Tell them they can go to a museum and see the jewelry, headdresses, and even the toys of the Egyptians. Make sure the children know these were real people.

For the fourth verse talk about what a person might do who finds a lost child.

The fifth verse gives you an opportunity to talk about where royalty lives. Because of the many Disney movies and fairytales featuring princesses, many children know the name of the place where a princess lives. However, most of them don't really know what a palace or castle is like. Here is an opportunity to tell them about it. Also, tell them they can go to Egypt and visit the land where Moses grew up. Show them photos of the pyramids. Work on pyramid shapes. Build a pyramid of blocks or other materials. Talk about the slaves who built them. What is a slave? How are they treated? Remind them that slavery is still alive in the world and that there were slaves in this country not too long ago. Teach them that this story reminds us that, not only do we never want to be slaves again, but that we never want to make others slaves.

The sixth verse is a fine time to talk with the children about growing up! They were babies once, though they might not want to admit it! With older children you can discuss the fact that Moses did not grow up as a slave. Because of this he was able to recognize the cruelty of slavery and also have the mental and physical strength to do something about the terrible situation of his people.

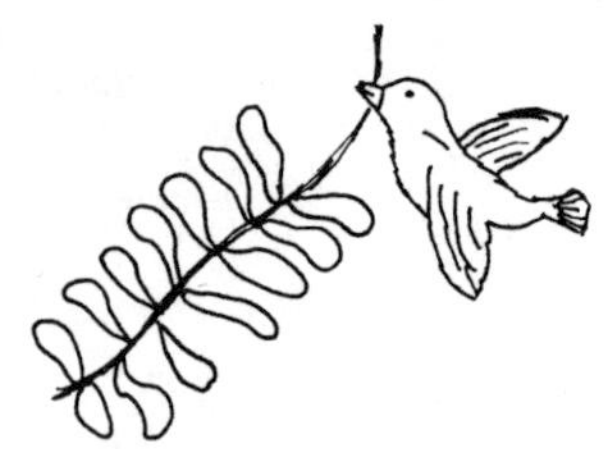

Chad Gadya (One Kid)

חַד גַּדְיָא

European Jewish Pesach song
from the Pesach Haggadah, in Aramaic

sung joyfully in a medium tempo;
speeding up as the verses get longer

Ab - ba bought for two zu - zey, Chad gad - ya,

chad gad - ya. Then came a stick, that beat the dog, that

bit the cat, that de - voured the kid, that my Ab - ba bought for

two zu - zey, Chad gad - ya, chad gad - ya. etc.

❉ Ossia (Frill)

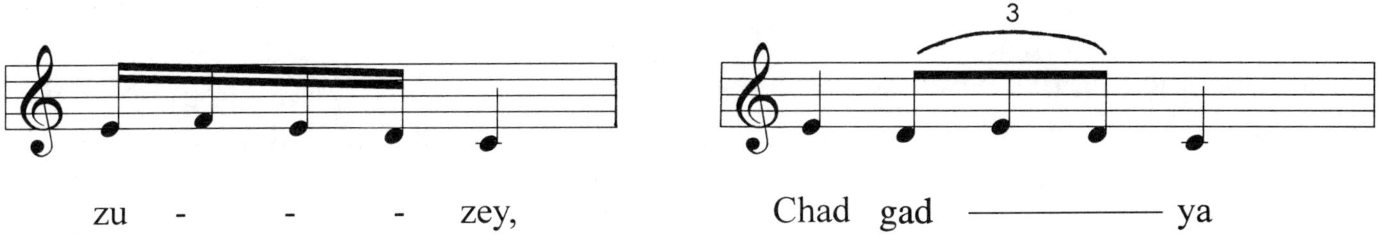
3
zu - - - zey,
Chad gad ya

**LYRICS IN ENGLISH (with a little Aramaic):

**LYRICS IN ARAMAIC:

Chorus:

That my father bought for two zuzey,
(two zuzey is like two dollars)
Chad gadya, chad gadya.
(One kid, one kid.)

פִּזְמוֹן:

דְּזַבִּן אַבָּא בִּתְרֵי זוּזֵי.

חַד גַּדְיָא חַד גַּדְיָא:

or:

D^{e}zabin abba bitrey zuzey,
Chad gadya, chad gadya.
sing it either way - I think it is more fun and sounds better to sing it in Aramaic!

דְּזַבִּן אַבָּא בִּתְרֵי זוּזֵי.
חַד גַּדְיָא חַד גַּדְיָא:

2) Then came a cat, that devoured the kid,
D^{e}zabin abba bitrey zuzey,
Chad gadya, chad gadya.

וְאָתָא שׁוּנְרָא. וְאָכְלָה לְגַדְיָא.
דְּזַבִּן אַבָּא בִּתְרֵי זוּזֵי.
חַד גַּדְיָא חַד גַּדְיָא:

3) Then came a dog, that bit the cat,
That devoured the kid,
D^{e}zabin abba bitrey zuzey,
Chad gadya, chad gadya.

וְאָתָא כַלְבָּא. וְנָשַׁךְ לְשׁוּנְרָא.
דְּאָכְלָה לְגַדְיָא.
דְּזַבִּן אַבָּא בִּתְרֵי זוּזֵי.
חַד גַּדְיָא חַד גַּדְיָא:

4) Then came a stick, that beat the dog,
That bit the cat, that devoured the kid,
D^{e}zabin Abba bitrey zuzey,
Chad gadya, chad gadya.

וְאָתָא חוּטְרָא. וְהִכָּה לְכַלְבָּא.
דְּנָשַׁךְ לְשׁוּנְרָא. דְּאָכְלָה לְגַדְיָא.
דְּזַבִּן אַבָּא בִּתְרֵי זוּזֵי.
חַד גַּדְיָא חַד גַּדְיָא:

5) Then came the fire, that burnt the stick,
That beat the dog, that bit the cat,
That devoured the kid,
D^{e}zabin Abba bitrey zuzey,
Chad gadya, chad gadya.

וְאָתָא נוּרָא. וְשָׂרַף לְחוּטְרָא.
דְּהִכָּה לְכַלְבָּא. דְּנָשַׁךְ לְשׁוּנְרָא.
דְּאָכְלָה לְגַדְיָא.
דְּזַבִּן אַבָּא בִּתְרֵי זוּזֵי.
חַד גַּדְיָא חַד גַּדְיָא:

6) Then came the water, that extinguished the fire,
That burnt the stick, that beat the dog,
That bit the cat, that devoured the kid,
D^{e}zabin Abba bitrey zuzey,
Chad gadya, chad gadya.

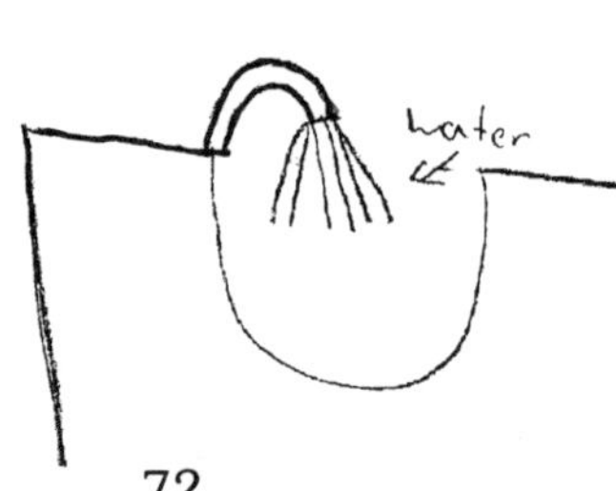

וְאָתָא מַיָּא. וְכָבָה לְנוּרָא.
דְּשָׂרַף לְחוּטְרָא. דְּהִכָּה לְכַלְבָּא.
דְּנָשַׁךְ לְשׁוּנְרָא. דְּאָכְלָה לְגַדְיָא.
דְּזַבִּן אַבָּא בִּתְרֵי זוּזֵי.
חַד גַּדְיָא חַד גַּדְיָא:

7) Then came the ox, that drank the water,
That extinguished the fire, that burnt the stick,
That beat the dog, that bit the cat,
That devoured the kid,
D^e^zabin Abba bitrey zuzey,
Chad gadya, chad gadya.

וְאָתָא תוֹרָא. וְשָׁתָא לְמַיָּא.
דְּכָבָה לְנוּרָא. דְּשָׂרַף לְחוּטְרָא.
דְּהִכָּה לְכַלְבָּא. דְּנָשַׁךְ לְשׁוּנְרָא.
דְּאָכְלָה לְגַדְיָא.
דְּזַבִּן אַבָּא בִּתְרֵי זוּזֵי.
חַד גַּדְיָא חַד גַּדְיָא:

8) Then came the butcher,
Who slaughtered the ox,
That drank the water, that extinguished the fire,
That burnt the stick, that beat the dog,
That bit the cat, that devoured the kid,
D^e^zabin Abba bitrey zuzey,
Chad gadya, chad gadya.

וְאָתָא הַשּׁוֹחֵט.
וְשָׁחַט לְתוֹרָא.
דְּשָׁתָא לְמַיָּא. דְּכָבָה לְנוּרָא.
דְּשָׂרַף לְחוּטְרָא. דְּהִכָּה לְכַלְבָּא.
דְּנָשַׁךְ לְשׁוּנְרָא. דְּאָכְלָה לְגַדְיָא.
דְּזַבִּן אַבָּא בִּתְרֵי זוּזֵי.
חַד גַּדְיָא חַד גַּדְיָא:

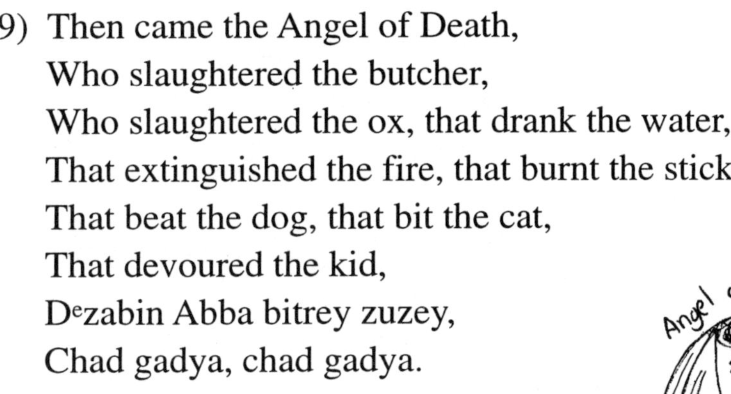

9) Then came the Angel of Death,
Who slaughtered the butcher,
Who slaughtered the ox, that drank the water,
That extinguished the fire, that burnt the stick,
That beat the dog, that bit the cat,
That devoured the kid,
D^e^zabin Abba bitrey zuzey,
Chad gadya, chad gadya.

וְאָתָא מַלְאַךְ הַמָּוֶת.
וְשָׁחַט לְשׁוֹחֵט.
דְּשָׁחַט לְתוֹרָא. דְּשָׁתָא לְמַיָּא.
דְּכָבָה לְנוּרָא. דְּשָׂרַף לְחוּטְרָא.
דְּהִכָּה לְכַלְבָּא. דְּנָשַׁךְ לְשׁוּנְרָא.
דְּאָכְלָה לְגַדְיָא.
דְּזַבִּן אַבָּא בִּתְרֵי זוּזֵי.
חַד גַּדְיָא חַד גַּדְיָא:

10) Then came haKodesh Baruch Hu,
Who slaughtered the Angel of Death,
Who slaughtered the butcher,
Who slaughtered the ox,
That drank the water, that extinguished the fire,
That burnt the stick, that beat the dog,
That bit the cat, that devoured the kid,
D^e^zabin Abba bitrey zuzey,
Chad gadya, chad gadya.

וְאָתָא הַקָּדוֹשׁ בָּרוּךְ הוּא.
וְשָׁחַט לְמַלְאַךְ הַמָּוֶת.
דְּשָׁחַט לְשׁוֹחֵט.
דְּשָׁחַט לְתוֹרָא.
דְּשָׁתָא לְמַיָּא. דְּכָבָה לְנוּרָא.
דְּשָׂרַף לְחוּטְרָא. דְּהִכָּה לְכַלְבָּא.
דְּנָשַׁךְ לְשׁוּנְרָא. דְּאָכְלָה לְגַדְיָא.
דְּזַבִּן אַבָּא בִּתְרֵי זוּזֵי.
חַד גַּדְיָא חַד גַּדְיָא:

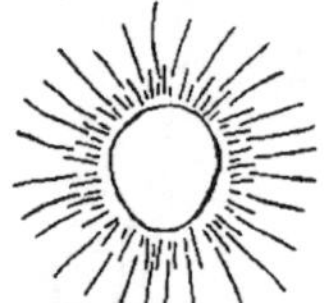  

This is the last song sung at the *Seder* table. Of Western European origin, and similar in form to folk songs of many cultures, it is from the oldest section of the *Haggadah*. Although the exact connection to the *Seder* is unclear, it is much loved by children (it was one of my favorite parts of the *Seder* and always brought everyone back to the table). As for what it's about, it seems to be an allegory: "Israel is the kid which God bought for two *zuzim,* the two tablets of the Covenant. Subsequently, Israel fell prey to the first series of empires, each of which destroyed its predecessor in turn. The cat is Assyria, the dog is Babylonia, the stick Persia, the fire Macedonia, the water Rome, the ox the Saracens, the butcher the crusaders, and the Angel of Death the Turks."* Most powerful of all, of course, is God.

Singing Games:

Younger children:

Sing the song as a "Farmer in the Dell" type game. Everyone holds hands and makes a circle. One person goes in the middle and is the kid. All sing,

"There was a kid–"

Here stop circling and begin clapping a strong, steady beat as you sing in English or Aramaic:

"that my father bought for two zuzey,
Chad gadya, chad gadya."

Then the kid picks a 'cat.' The person who is the cat joins the kid in the middle of the circle as everyone else sings as they walk round and round.

"Then came a cat that devoured the kid–"

Here stop circling and begin clapping a strong, steady beat as you sing in English or Aramaic:

That my father bought for two zuzey,
Chad gadya, chad gadya."

Remember to stop circling and clap hands as the chorus is sung. The person who is the 'cat' picks someone to be a 'dog.' The 'dog' joins the others in the middle as everyone else sings and circles around.

"Then came a dog that bit the cat
That devoured the kid–"

Here stop circling and begin clapping a strong, steady beat as you sing in English or Aramaic:

That my father bought for two zuzey,
Chad gadya, chad gadya."

Continue in this way until all the characters of the story are in the middle of the circle. If your *Seder* isn't big enough to accommodate all the characters, next year invite more people!

*From *The Passover Haggadah,* based on the commentaries of E. D. Goldschmidt, edited by Nahum N. Glazer, Schocken Books, New York, 1979.

Another way to enjoy this song is to find props that represent the characters, such as stuffed or plastic animals for the animal characters, colored scarves for the water and fire, a knife made out of a stick with a piece of foil attached to it, and so on. Let the children help you gather the props or make them. At the *Seder* hand them out, putting the characters next to each other at the table or in a line. As you sing the song have each person make his prop move in a way that expresses the action of the song.

Older children:

With older children it is fun, first of all, to learn the song! It is a challenge to the memory and speech coordination. See if they can sing the last verse on one breath. Have a kind of singing race and see who can sing the last verse fastest, without making a mistake of course! Doing this in Aramaic would be even more of a challenge and sounds better, too.

Discussion Topics:

Teachers and parents have expressed their concern to me about the violence in this song. They felt some children would be frightened by it. Although the song has generated questions from young children, after talking about what frightened them they had no trouble continuing to sing it and play the circle game. In fact the violence children see on television and hear about inadvertently is far more horrible. Chad Gadya is like a good fairytale - it is inscrutable, a little scary, and the good king is strongest. Regarding the Angel of Death, my experience has been that singing this part of the song helps children talk about death. Many children have had experiences with either the death of a relative or a pet, and don't get enough opportunity to talk about it. Songs help children recognize their feelings, express them, and understand them. Music helps children realize that they are not the only ones who have felt frightened or confused, sad or alone, happy, silly, or safe.

The image of death many children have is that of a horrible creature. This song affords us the chance to tell children that death can also be gentle; an animal or person can peacefully die in their sleep.

Lastly, Chad Gadya is part of the *Seder* tradition. It is no more violent than the Pesach story itself or any of the other holiday stories, so many of which involve cruel injustice or the real threat of death. If a child is ready to learn why baby Moses' mother had to hide him, what the tenth plague was, why Haman was so bad, or why the Maccabees fought Antiochus, they are ready to sing this song. We must look at this tradition of fighting against injustice and cruelty and take our lesson from that. We should ask ourselves how we can teach our children to help make the world a more just and peaceful place.

Eliahu haNavi (Elijah the Prophet)

אֵלִיָּהוּ הַנָּבִיא

European Jewish folk song

**TRANSLITERATED HEBREW LYRICS:

Eliahu haNavi, Eliahu haTishbi,
Eliahu, Eliahu, Eliahu haGiladi,
Eliahu, Eliahu, Eliahu haGiladi.
Bimherah v'yameynu,
Yavo eyleynu
Im Mashiach, ben David,
Im Mashiach, ben David.
Eliahu haNavi, Eliahu haTishbi,
Eliahu, Eliahu, Eliahu haGiladi,
Eliahu, Eliahu, Eliahu haGiladi.

**LYRICS IN HEBREW:

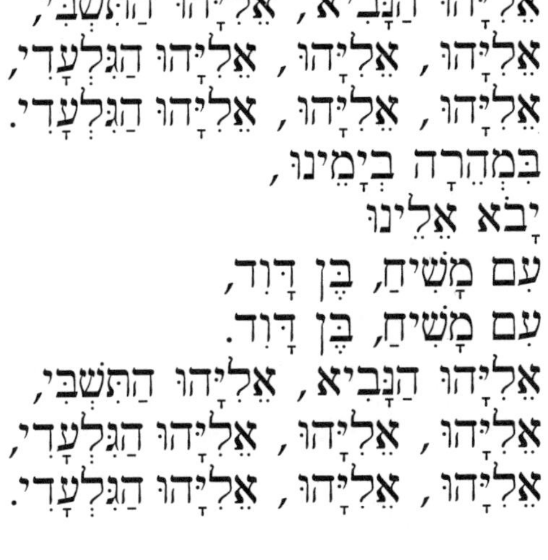
אֵלִיָּהוּ הַנָּבִיא, אֵלִיָּהוּ הַתִּשְׁבִּי,
אֵלִיָּהוּ, אֵלִיָּהוּ, אֵלִיָּהוּ הַגִּלְעָדִי,
אֵלִיָּהוּ, אֵלִיָּהוּ, אֵלִיָּהוּ הַגִּלְעָדִי.
בִּמְהֵרָה בְיָמֵינוּ,
יָבֹא אֵלֵינוּ
עִם מָשִׁיחַ, בֶּן דָּוִד,
עִם מָשִׁיחַ, בֶּן דָּוִד.
אֵלִיָּהוּ הַנָּבִיא, אֵלִיָּהוּ הַתִּשְׁבִּי,
אֵלִיָּהוּ, אֵלִיָּהוּ, אֵלִיָּהוּ הַגִּלְעָדִי,
אֵלִיָּהוּ, אֵלִיָּהוּ, אֵלִיָּהוּ הַגִּלְעָדִי.

TRANSLATION OF HEBREW LYRICS:

Elijah the Prophet, Elijah the Tishbite,
Elijah, Elijah, Elijah of Gilad,
Elijah, Elijah, Elijah of Gilad.
Speedily and in our time,
May he come to us
With the Messiah, son of David,
With the Messiah, son of David.

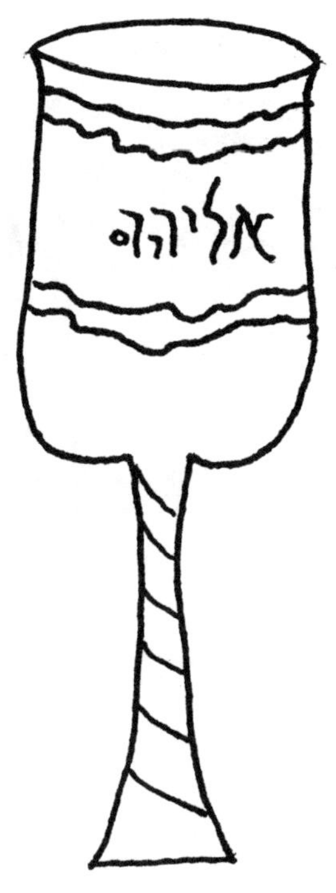

Sing this song with children when they need a quiet, restful atmosphere. If it is part of your classroom style, let them lie down while they listen to this song. After you have sung it to them once or twice, ask them to help you sing it. Even the youngest children at school (babies of 18 months!) derive great pleasure from the soothing melody and the open vowel sounds of the lyrics, especially in the name Eliahu. I have found that they will begin singing along right away.

The song is sung during the *Seder,* after the third cup of wine is drunk and after the verses beginning, "Pour out Your wrath on the nations that know You not." Before these words are said it is traditional to have the children in the family open the front door of the house to welcome Elijah the Prophet to come in and drink from his cup at the table. I remember how apprehensive I felt as a child opening the door into the dark night. The cool air from outside would rush onto my face and into my nose, sharp and clear; the warmth and savory smells of the house, the light and the merry voices, all seemed to urge me forward and yet protect me from whatever waited out in the night to come in. For me this was the most mysterious, scary, and wonderful part of the *Seder.*

This song is also sung on Saturday evenings at the departure of *Shabbat* (the Sabbath).

Yom haSho-ah

יוֹם הַשּׁוֹאָה

and

Yom ha-Atzma-ut

יוֹם הָעַצְמָאוּת

Holiday:

Yom haSho-ah (Holocaust Remembrance Day, in April or May, 5 days after Passover ends) **and Yom ha-Atzma-ut** (Israeli Independence Day, in April or May, about two weeks after Passover ends):

What are they about?

Both are historical holidays. The first commemorates the Holocaust, the second celebrates the day when Israel became a modern nation. In the Jewish calendar the latter is the 5th day of the month of Iyyar.

How are they celebrated?

Holocaust Remembrance Day is marked with memorial services for all ages, including commemorations suitable for children. In Israel, a siren blasts for one minute and everyone stops what they are doing, even driving, and stands still and silent. On Independence Day there are parties in the streets, parades, dancing and singing. The day before *(Yom haZikaron)* there are memorial services for those who fell in Israel's wars.

Interdisciplinary ideas:

Geography:

Show the children a globe. Find Israel. Do comparisons of size and location with Israel and the city and country the children live in. Get illustrated books about Israel that tell about her geography. Most large synagogues have these books in their libraries. Show them pictures. Talk about the climate, the desert, the Dead Sea, the Mediterranean Sea, the different people from all over the world who live in Israel.

History:

How does one introduce the Holocaust to young children? I have been grappling with this question for some time both as a teacher and as a parent. One thing is for certain: Yom haSho-ah should not go untaught, even to young children as long as we teach them about it in a manner that suits their age. The National Holocaust Museum in Washington, D.C. does this with "Daniel's Story."

If we don't begin this education, developing an appreciation of pre-War European Jewish life, then learning about the Holocaust becomes a study only in horrors and unimaginable statistics, unconnected to real lives. By bringing these lost lives, with the emphasis on *lives*, to the attention of our children, we assure that those lives will not be forgotten, belittled, or denied.

As I explain below, there are many ways to introduce children to European Jewish culture. This should be done all year, not just at this time; this is the most essential thing about beginning to teach the Holocaust, no matter the age group. As to how I have approached the actual destruction of the Jews and their culture, it has been, as always, the children I taught who showed me what to do.

We had been learning all year about various Jewish holidays, and in doing so learning about the adversaries and heroes of each. The Maccabees and Antiochus, Esther and Mordecai and Haman, Moses and Pharaoh. For Yom haSho-ah we have a similar situation, only it is in our time. The adversary was Hitler and all those who followed his ideas. So I tell the children, "There was a man who hated Jewish people, just like Haman did, who didn't want them to celebrate their holidays just like King Antiocus did, and who made them slaves just like Pharaoh did. His name was Hitler. He lived in Germany, in Europe, not very long ago, but he's dead now." *(The children always want to know for sure that Hitler is dead now. If they ask if he'll come back I say, we have to guard against someone like him or other 'bad guys' arising by always standing up for what we know is right and being ready to fight for what is right.*) "Hitler had many people to help him do these terrible things." (*Here a discussion often ensues regarding the power of one bad person. The children need to realize that one bad person can't do much harm on his or her own; it is only when they have a lot of support that they become dangerous to everyone. This is a time to talk about standing up for what you know is right, even when you see people all around you doing something else and telling you to do it too, even though it is wrong.*) "Hitler, like Pharaoh, was especially cruel to Jewish children."

(*As an introduction to singing "Michalke" you can say:*)

"These children were just like you. They liked to play and sing and make believe. Here's a song they sang when they were playing a make-believe game about instruments." (*Then sing the song.*)

"Some of the parents of these children who lived in Europe decided to save their children from Hitler and his helpers. They put their children on boats and planes and trains, and some of them even had to walk, and these children were taken to other countries where they would be safe. Some came to America, some went to England or South America or South Africa, but many went to Israel."

"When they got to Israel they had a problem. They couldn't understand each other! All the children came from different countries, and though many of them spoke Yiddish" (*see notes below about introducing the children to Yiddish*), "they also spoke other languages, such as French and Italian, Hungarian and Russian, Polish and..." (*great moment for a geography lesson*). "So they all had to learn the same language because there was a lot of work to be done to build their new country. Do you know what language they learned? Hebrew." (*If you are talking to Jewish kids you can give them a hint such as: you already know some words in this language, like Chanukah and Shabbat and challah and baruch ata [which means 'blessed are you']...*)

Then you can sing songs in Hebrew. (In addition to the songs in this book, see the 'music' section on the next page and look in the books in the Music Resources section.)

Language:

Help the children (and their parents) become aware of all the Yiddish words they already know, such as:

bagel (a chewy, doughnut-shaped bread that is first boiled, then baked)
kugel (a baked dish made primarily of noodles)
latkes (potato pancakes fried in oil, eaten especially on Chanukah)
rugelech (rolled cookies filled with cinnamon, raisins, and nuts)
dreydl (a specially marked spinning top used on Chanukah)
gelt (it means money, but is used most frequently to refer to the money, both real and chocolate, that children receive on Chanukah)
grogger (the noise maker used for Purim)
homentashn (the stuffed cookies eaten on Purim; named after the evil Haman)
gezuntheit (good health; said after someone sneezes)
bubbe (grandma) and *zayde* (grandpa)
bubbele (darling; a term of endearment)
mazel tov (congratulations; from Hebrew for good luck or good fortune)
meshugene (crazy or going crazy)
potsch (what you get on your tuches!)
pupik (bellybutton)
shlep (to drag around or carry from here to there and there to here)
shmaltz (fat, such as chicken fat, but also emotional sentimentality)
shmate (rag)
shmutz (dirt)
shooz (chat)
shpil (the whole story)
tuches (American version - tushi; comes from the Hebrew word - tachat, which means bottom, and affectionately refers to that part of our anatomy)
tsures (troubles)
yente (a gossip) . . . and so on.

You'd be surprised how many words people already know, including those that are not so nice!

Literature:

It is most important that children begin to appreciate the rich, varied and highly sophisticated Jewish culture that existed in Europe before World War II. As they grow and can start to learn what happened just before and during the war, they will experience the great loss all Jews, and all people, suffer. Begin by reading stories from the *shtetl* (the small, segregated Jewish villages of Europe). Most large synagogues have libraries with a good children's collection. The various Chelm stories, about a town of fools, as well as many others that have been recently adapted by popular children's authors, are fun to read, well-illustrated and present a dynamic picture of European Jewish life.

Look at photos of the *shtetls* and the people who lived in them, such as those taken by Roman Vishnaic. His books are easy to find in major bookstores and in libraries. There are also photos of the synagogues of Berlin, where Jews were as much a part of urban life as they are in New York, and photos of the Jewish quarter of Prague or Venice. These books teach children about other lands and also give them a strong sense of how much a part of the life of these cities Jews were. Some of the places shown in these books can still be visited today. Children should know that too. When they are older they will find out how altered those places are.

Music:

For Yom haSho-ah: Listen to *klezmer* music, an irresistible music that combines traditional Jewish musical styles with the music of Russian, Polish, Rumanian, and other European peoples as well. American *klezmer* music was much influenced by jazz and the Yiddish theatre in America. Wherever Jews lived they adopted and adapted the music of the non-Jews they lived among. Learn a few songs in Yiddish (try those included in this book as well as *"Chanukah Oy! Chanukah")*. Yiddish is a Germanic language and close to English. It is much easier to learn a song in Yiddish than in Hebrew for those who are unfamiliar with both languages.

For Israel Independence Day one of the best songs for children is, "Beautiful Yisrael" by Leah Abrams (see Music Resources section). Sing songs from the pioneer days of Israel, such as *"Tsena, Tsena," "Artsa Alinu," "Erets Zavat Chalav," "Kadima haPoel," "Zum Gali, Gali,"* and so on. Ella Jenkins sings several of these old Israeli songs on her recordings; on the harmonica she plays a haunting version of the Yiddish theatre song, *"Rozhinkes mit Mandlen"* ("Raisins and Almonds").

These old songs have strong rhythms, simple words with a lot of repetition, and melodies that make you want to sing them. They are easy to find in songbooks. You can feel the hope of the people who wrote these songs, as well as their hard work and sorrow. They clearly express the happiness these people felt at finally being free to be Jews without oppression, but also reveal their suffering, their uncertainty about the future, and their sadness at leaving friends and family behind. The melodies are a dynamic mixture of Middle Eastern and European folk music. The young people who came to settle Israel clearly were enamored of their new land and the music they found there, but they carried with them the beautiful traditions of European music. They combined the two lovingly and in powerful balance.

Social Studies:

A great way to celebrate Israeli Independence Day is by eating some of the typical foods of Israel. The most fun to prepare and eat is *falafel* stuffed in pita, a "fast food" eaten throughout the Middle East. *Falafel* are balls made from ground chickpeas and seasonings fried in oil. *Pita* is a round pocket bread. The *falafel* are stuffed into the *pita* with a few tomatoes or strips of lettuce and topped with a white sesame sauce or a hot sauce. You can also bring in some of the fruits grown in Israel to reinforce what was learned on Tu BiShvat. This would include all kinds of citrus fruits, almonds and sesame seeds, chickpeas, avocados, grapes, olives, figs, and dates. Older children can do research to find out what produce is grown, what kinds of animals are raised, and what industrial products are made in Israel.

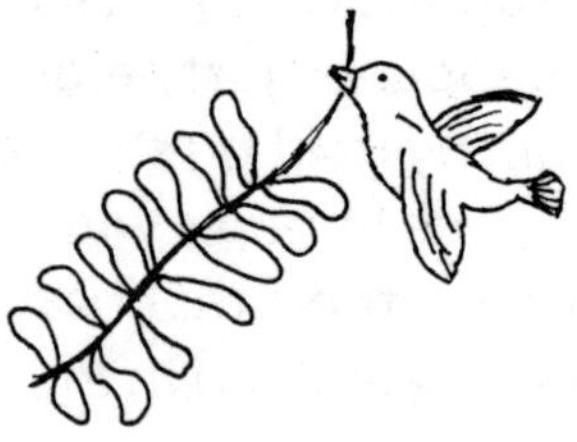

Michalke

מיכאַלקע

Yiddish folk song
English lyrics (inspired by Ruth Rubin)
by Rachel Buchman
Happy Valley Music, BMI
(T. J. F.)

playfully in a
medium tempo

F
I have a friend called Mi-chal-ke, Mi-chal-ke. He

G7 C7
lives on the big main street. He makes me

F C7 F
what I want, He makes me what he can,

G7 C7 F G7 C7
He makes me an or-ches-tra and the whis-tle sounds like

F F
this: (Chorus:) Flu-flu-flu, – Flu-flu-flu, –

2. the

1. G7 C7 F
That's how the whis-tle blew!

2. G7 C7 F
whis-tle sounds like this!*

In Yiddish:

*As you add instruments, repeat the chorus singing all the previous instrument sounds from most recently added, backwards to the first sound.

**ENGLISH LYRICS:

1) I have a friend called Michalke, Michalke.
He lives on the big main street.
He makes me what I want,
He makes me what he can,
He makes me an orchestra
And the whistle sounds like this:
Flu-flu-flu, flu-flu-flu,
That's how the whistle blew,
Flu-flu-fu, flu-flu-flu
The whistle sounds like this.

2) I have a friend called Michalke, Michalke.
He lives on the big main street.
He makes me what I want,
He makes me what he can,
He makes me an orchestra
And the bugle sounds like this:
Tru-tru-tru, tru-tru-tru,
That's how the bugle blew,
Tru-tru-tru, tru-tru-tru,
The bugle sounds like this.

3) I have a friend called Michalke, Michalke.
He lives on the big main street.
He makes me what I want,
He makes me what he can
He makes me an orchestra
And the drum sounds like this:
Rrram-pam-pam, rrram-pam-pam,
That's how he plays the drum,
Rrram-pam-pam, rrram-pam-pam,
The drum sounds like this.

additional instruments:

4) And the cymbals sound like this:
Tsim-tsim-tsim, tsim-tsim-tsim,
That's how the cymbals clang,
Tsim-tsim-tsim, tsim-tsim-tsim,
The cymbals sound like this.

5) And the fiddle sounds like this:
Feedl-deedl-deedl, feedl-deedl-dee,
That's how he plays for me,
Feedl-deedl-deedl, feedl-deedl-dee,
The fiddle sounds like this.

**TRANSLITERATED YIDDISH LYRICS:

1) Hob ich mir a kleynem
Michalke, Michalke.
Voynt er oyf der langer gas.
Macht er mir vos ich vil,
Macht er mir vos er kon,
Macht er mir a fayfele,
Dos fayfele macht azoy!
Flu-fu-flu, flu-flu-flu,
Azoy macht dos fayfele,
Flu-flu-flu, flu-flu-flu,
Dos fayfele macht azoy!

**LYRICS IN YIDDISH:

האָב איך מיר אַ קליינעם
מיכאַלקע, מיכאַלקע.
וווינט ער אויף דער לאַנגער גאַס.
מאַכט ער מיר וואָס איך וויל,
מאַכט ער מיר וואָס ער קאָן,
מאַכט ער מיר אַ פֿײַפֿעלע,
דאָס פֿייפֿעלע מאַכט אַזוי!
פֿלו-פֿלו-פֿלו, פֿלו-פֿלו-פֿלו,
אַזוי מאַכט דאָס פֿײַפֿעלע,
פֿלו-פֿלו-פֿלו, פֿלו-פֿלו-פֿלו,
דאָס פֿייפֿעלע מאַכט אַזוי!

2) Hob ich mir a kleynem
Michalke, Michalke.
Voynt er oyf der langer gas.
Macht er mir vos ich vil,
Macht er mir vos er kon,
Macht er mir a trubetske,
Dos trubetske macht azoy!
Tru-tru-tru, tru-tru-tru,
Azoy macht dos trubetske,
Tru-tru-tru, tru-tru-tru,
Dos trubetske macht azoy!

האָב איך מיר אַ קליינעם
מיכאַלקע, מיכאַלקע.
וווינט ער אויף דער לאַנגער גאַס.
מאַכט ער מיר וואָס איך וויל,
מאַכט ער מיר וואָס ער קאָן,
מאַכט ער מיר אַ טרובעצקע
דאָס טרובעצקע מאַכט אַזוי!
טרו-טרו-טרו, טרו-טרו-טרו,
אזוי מאַכט דאָס טרובעצקע,
טרו-טרו-טרו, טרו-טרו-טרו,
דאָס טרובעצקע מאַכט אַזוי!

3) *(same first four lines)*
Macht er mir a paykele,
Dos paykele macht azoy!
Tara-bam-bam-bam, tara-bam-bam-bam,

Azoy macht dos paykele,
Tara-bam-bam-bam, tara-bam-bam-bam,

Dos paykele macht azoy!

(same first four lines)
מאַכט ער מיר אַ פּײַקעלע
דאָס פּײַקעלע מאַכט אַזוי!
טאַראַ-באַם-באַם-באַם,
טאַראַ-באַם-באַם-באַם
אזוי מאַכט דאָס פּײַקעלע
טאַראַ-באַם-באַם-באַם,
טאַראַ-באַם-באַם-באַם
דאָס פּײַקעלע מאַכט אַזוי!

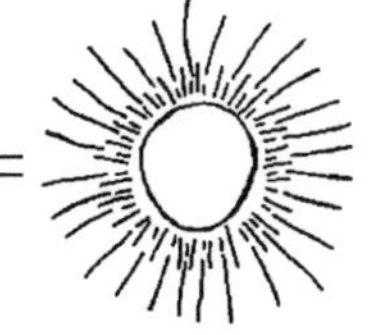

Musical Activity:

More instruments: *tsimbele* - צימבעלע - cymbals sounds like this: *tzim-tzim-tzim; fidele* - פידעלע - fiddle sounds like this: *fidl-didl-didl* (or have the children make up their own sound effects and hand motions).

Have the children 'blow' the whistle *(fifele* - פּײַפעלע) or bugle *(trubetske* - טרובעצקע) by tooting, 'beat' the drums by stamping their feet, and 'bang' the cymbals by clapping their hands together with big circular motions. First have them do each instrument alone. Then, for the last verse (in English) when you make a whole orchestra, have them 'play' all the instruments at the same time! So they'll be tooting, stamping, and clapping simultaneously. This is great fun and great for their coordination too.!

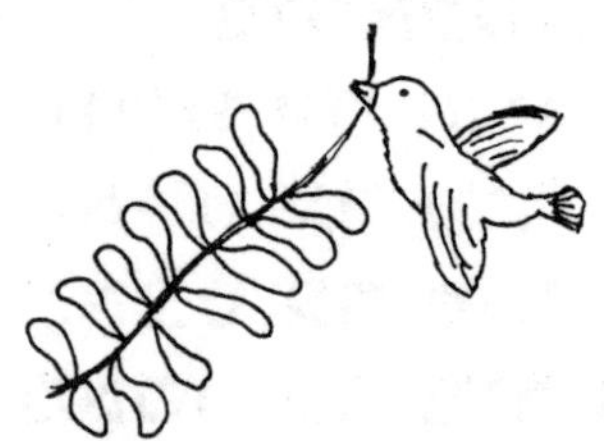

Simi Yadech b^{e}Yadi (Put Your Hand in Mine)

שִׂמִי יָדֵךְ בְּיָדִי

Israeli folk song
English lyrics and dance by Rachel Buchman
Happy Valley Music, BMI
(N.C.S.)

lighthearted, medium tempo

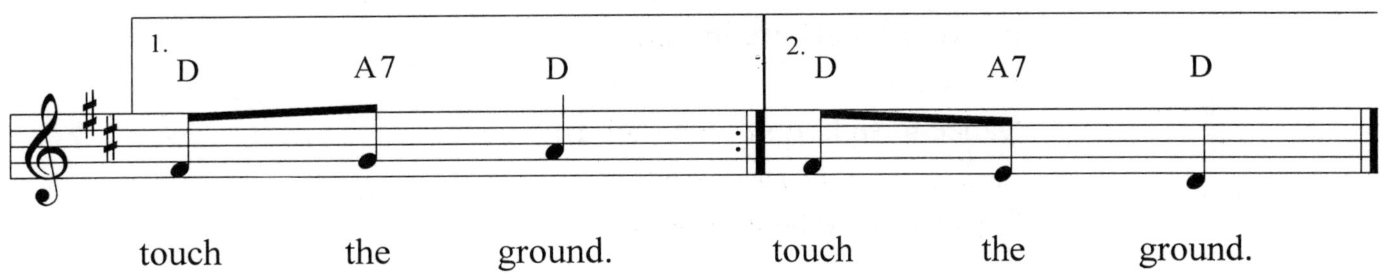

**1) Put your hand here in mine,
Dance to the right, don't we look fine?
Put your hand here in mine,
Dance to the left, don't we look fine?
Hey! Hey! Galiyah,
Bat harim yefefiyah!
Hey! Hey! Galiyah,
Bat harim yefefiyah!

2) Simi yadech b^{e}yadi,
Ani shelach v^{e}at sheli.
Simi yadech b^{e}yadi,
Ani shelach v^{e}at sheli.
Hey! Hey! Dance around,
Our feet will hardly touch the ground.
Hey! Hey! Dance around,
Our feet will hardly touch the ground.

You can do a dance figure with this song:

Have everyone make a circle. Drop hands and sing:
Put your hand here in mine,
take hands
Dance to right don't we look fine.
circle to the right. Drop hands
Put your hand here in mine,
take hands
Dance to the left, don't we look fine.
circle to the left
Hey! Hey! Dance around,
take four steps into the middle
Our feet will hardly touch the ground.
take four steps out
Hey! Hey! Dance around,
take four steps into the middle
Our feet will hardly touch the ground.
take four steps out

Vary the pattern by hopping, tiptoeing, or skipping when you circle round: "hop to the right" or "skip to the right," etc. For younger children, once hands are taken don't drop hands to change directions from right to left around the circle. Simply circle to the left when you begin the second repetition of "Put your hand here in mine."

TRANSLATION OF HEBREW:

Put your hand in mine,
I am yours and you are mine.
(repeat)
Hey! Hey! Girl of the Galil,
Beautiful daughter of the mountains.
(repeat)

**LYRICS IN HEBREW:

שִׂמִי יָדֵךְ בְּיָדִי
אֲנִי שֶׁלָּךְ וְאַתְּ שֶׁלִּי.
(עוֹד הַפַּעַם)
הֵי, הֵי גַּלְיָה,
בַּת הָרִים יְפֵהפִיָּה.
(עוֹד הַפַּעַם)

The original Hebrew version of this song is a longer, light-hearted love song from pre-State of Israel days. Here is a translation of those lyrics:

Why do I need champagne, and why rum?
Without you I have nothing.
I just saw you this evening
And fell head over heels in love with you.

Chorus:
Hey, hey Galiyah,
Beautiful daughter of the mountains.

Your eyes are like two doves.
Your lips like roses.
Your gentle arms
Were created only to embrace.

Hey, hey Galiyah...

Why do I need a father and why a mother?
For without you it is so boring!
Put your hand in mine
I am yours and you are mine.

Hey, hey Galiyah...

You are angry, my girl.
We'll be reconciled my lovely one.
My girl gave me her hand
And became mine forever.

Hey, hey Galiyah...

Yesh Li Pijama (I have Pajamas)

יֵשׁ לִי פִּיגָ׳מָה

(originally titled Kachol-Lavan, Blue-White / כָּחֹל-לָבָן)

by Leah Abrams

a medium swing tempo

**I have, I have pajamas,
I have, I have pajamas,
I have pajamas that are blue and white,
Blue and white, like -
The flag of Yisrael!

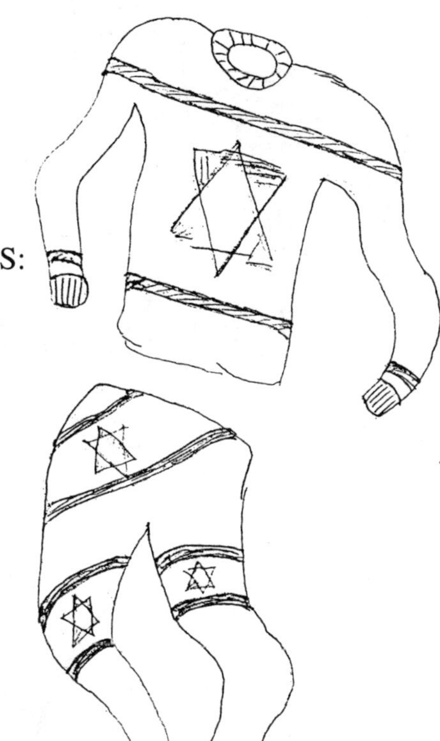

**TRANSLITERATION OF HEBREW LYRICS:

Yesh li, li pijama,
Yesh li, li pijama,
Yesh li pijama b^{e}kachol-lavan,
Kachol-lavan, k'mo-
Degel Yisrael!

**LYRICS IN HEBREW:

יֵשׁ לִי , לִי פִּיגָ׳מָה
יֵשׁ לִי , לִי פִּיגָ׳מָה
יֵשׁ לִ פִּגָ׳מָה בְּכָחֹל-לָבָן,
כָּחֹל-לָבָן כְּמוֹ-
דֶּגֶל יִשְׂרָאֵל!

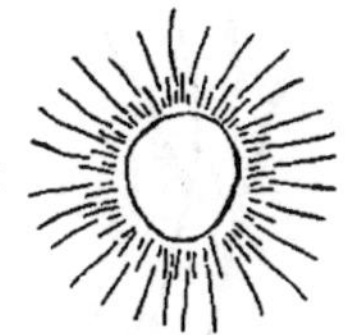

Musical Activity/Hebrew Game:

It is fun to add a sound effect to this song. The chords are reminiscent of early rock n'roll songs, so add a swinging "sh-tu, sh-sh-tu" (the sound of brushes on high-top cymbals!). With older children, have one group do the "sh-tu" as an intro to the song while the others sing the first two lines (the sound effect doesn't fit in with the rest of the song). Then all sing the last three lines. With younger children, have everyone sing the "sh-tu" intro and just sing the whole song afterwards. If the young children get very good at the song, you can try singing the back-up against their voices.

Teach the children the meaning of the words *kachol* and *lavan* (blue and white in Hebrew). Play a looking game: When you say *kachol* have the children look around the room, using only their eyes to find something blue. Then say *lavan* and ask the children to look for something white. Alternate between the colors as rapidly as the children can keep up with you. You can extend the game with older children, having them start at one spot and walking to the object they see that is blue or white. Play the game with some of these other words.

Here are a few other color words in Hebrew:

adom אָדוֹם (red)
tsahov צָהוֹב (yellow)
yarok יָרוֹק (green)
shachor שָׁחוֹר (black)

L'ag ba-Omer

לַ״ג בָּעֹמֶר

Holiday:

L'ag ba-Omer (literally the 33rd day of the counting of the Omer, in May)

What's it about?

A spiritual and historical holiday. "L'ag" is the alphabetical equivalent of the number 33.* An omer is an ancient dry measure of grain. The counting of the omer, which lasts for seven weeks, begins on the second night of Passover and concludes with Shavuot. It is a time to prepare for the giving of the Torah, a 'count-up' to one of the central events in human history. The counting is symbolic of the gradual change from a people enslaved to a people with laws, responsibilities, and their own relationship to God. The whole counting period of 49 days is considered one of semi-mourning – no weddings are celebrated during these 49 days, except on Lag b'Omer.

How is it celebrated?

The 33rd day of the counting is a day of celebration. It has a camp spirit to it, a holiday for picnics in the country, hikes, and bonfires. There are a few explanations for the happy atmosphere of this day; for instance, a plague that was killing many of Rabbi Akiba's students in the Second Century C.E., was lifted on this day.

*Each letter of the Hebrew alphabet, called the *aleph bet,* has a numerical equivalent. There is a complicated system of finding the numerical values of words and the spiritual connections they have with other words, called *gematria.*

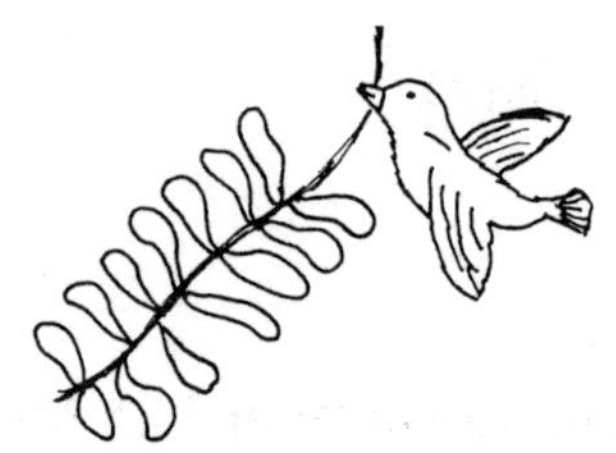

Esh, Esh (Fire, Fire)

אֵשׁ , אֵשׁ

Israeli folk song
English lyrics and dance by Rachel Buchman
Happy Valley Music, BMI
(S.C.)

start the dance slowly;
increase the tempo until
your circle whirls around!

Am Dm E
Fi - re, fi - re burn - ing bright, Dance a - round the

Am E7 Am Am Dm
fire to - night. Fi - re, fi - re burn - ing bright,

E7 Am Am
It's L'ag ba - O - mer! Esh, esh

Dm E Am E7 Am
me - du - rah Ho - rah, ho - rah mi - sa - viv,

Am Dm E7 Am E7 Am
Esh, esh me- du - rah L'ag ba - O- mer, chag cha- viv!

**ENGLISH LYRICS:

Fire, fire burning bright,
Dance around the fire tonight.
Fire, fire burning bright,
It's L'ag ba-Omer.

**TRANSLITERATED HEBREW LYRICS:

Esh, esh m^{e}durah
Horah, horah misaviv,
Esh, esh m^{e}durah
L'ag b^{e}Omer, chag chaviv.

Lai, lai, lai-lai lai...

**LYRICS IN HEBREW:

אֵשׁ , אֵשׁ מְדוּרָה,
הוֹרָה , הוֹרָה מִסָּבִיב!
אֵשׁ , אֵשׁ מְדוּרָה,
לַ״ג בָּעֹמֶר , חַג חָבִיב!

TRANSLATION OF HEBREW LYRICS:

Fire, fire, bonfire
Dance the horah* around
Fire, fire, bonfire
L'ag ba-Omer, lovely holiday!

*traditional Israeli circle dance

Do a simple dance with this song.

Hold hands and make a circle. Start singing the song slowly as you circle slowly around a make-believe fire. Each time you repeat a verse, make the circle go 'round a bit faster. Don't fall into the fire!

Shavuot

שָׁבוּעוֹת

Holiday:

Shavuot (literally, Weeks; also called the Feast of the First Fruits, or Feast of the Giving of the *Torah,* in May or June)

What's it about?

A historical, agricultural, and spiritual holiday. It commemorates God's giving of the Torah at Mount Sinai to Moses and the Children of Israel as well as the first harvest of the year, the first born animals of the year, originally designated to be brought to the Temple in Jerusalem for sacrifice. The word for week and the word for seven share the same root in Hebrew. The Children of Israel received the *Torah* only seven weeks after Pesach, seven weeks after their departure from Egypt and a life of slavery. As Moses soon found out, the people were barely ready to receive it!

Although it is a holiday of great significance, not just for Jews but for all people who regard the Ten Commandments as a guide for life, because of its position in the calendar it often falls at the end of the school year. It is a neglected and under-appreciated holiday!

How is it celebrated?

People attend synagogue, say special prayers, sing songs, eat a feast of dairy dishes, read the Book of Ruth. It is traditional to decorate the synagogue and home with green branches and flowers. It is customary to stay up the entire night of Shavuot to study and discuss the *Torah.* Singing songs helps everyone stay awake. Since there is no longer a sacrifice of first fruits, people today often make contributions of food to charitable organizations at this time.

Interdisciplinary ideas:

Literature:

An excellent book for children of all ages, *A Torah is Written* by Paul and Rachel Cowan, takes the reader through all the steps of preparing the scroll and writing it. The simple, clear text is illustrated with photographs. With younger children, only read part of the text. Read the children favorite Bible stories at this time of year. This will help them make the connection that these well-loved stories are from the *Torah* and receiving the *Torah* is what is being celebrated. For example: Peter Spier's *Noah's Ark* tells the whole story in pictures that bring tremendous life to the familiar story. It is not just a picturebook for young children. On the contrary older children will appreciate it even more. Have them read the original story and then look at Spier's book. This exercise will show them how much there is in the story for them to draw out. These illustrations serve a similar purpose to that of a *midrash* (an illuminating story based on a biblical word, phrase, character or story). Then let them pick a *Torah* story or event and illustrate it; guide them to add details of real life that will give the story sense.

Music:

Sing American songs about spring, baby animals, and planting. Sing songs such as "Joshua Fought the Battle of Jericho," "Who Built the Ark?" "Rise and Shine," "Who Did Swallow Jonah?" and other songs based on *Torah* stories.

Field Trips:

1) Find out if there is a *sofer (Torah* scribe) in your city or town. (You can get this information by calling the local *Chabad* House, a Lubavitch organization, or, if there is no *Chabad* House in your town or city, call a synagogue.) Take a field trip to visit the *sofer* and observe some of the work he does. 2) Visit a synagogue to see an unrolled *Torah* scroll. Have a rabbi show the children the way the *Torah* is dressed, rolled, and unrolled, and how it is read. If possible, have someone chant a little of it to them so they can hear how it sounds when it is read from the scroll. However be sure they understand that the stories from the *Torah* can also be read in letters they can read! Read them an illustrated book with a *Torah* story in it. 3) Visit a working farm where there are baby animals and where farmers can explain the planting/harvesting process in a way children understand.

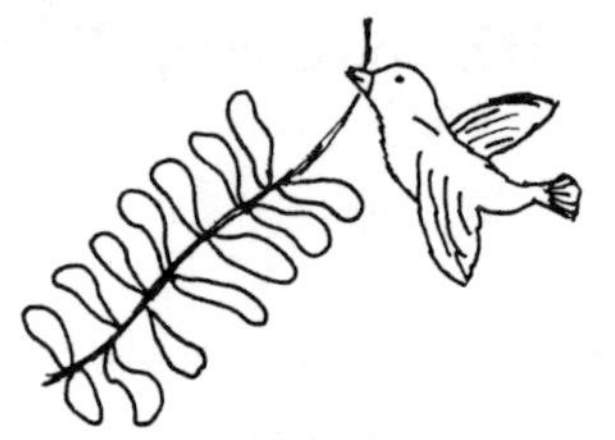

Spring Parade

(originally titled Saleynu, Our Baskets)

סַלֵּינוּ

music by J. Admon (Gorochov)
Hebrew lyrics by Levin-Kipnis, ACUM
English lyrics, except for first two lines,
by Rachel Buchman
(S.W.S.)

a joyful march

A Bm E7 A

We'll wel-come spring with har- vests, With the first things that grow.
Who brought it to us? Mo- she!* Where were we? Har Si - nai!*

A Em A

From the E - mek, Yer - u - sha - la - yim and Ri - shon,

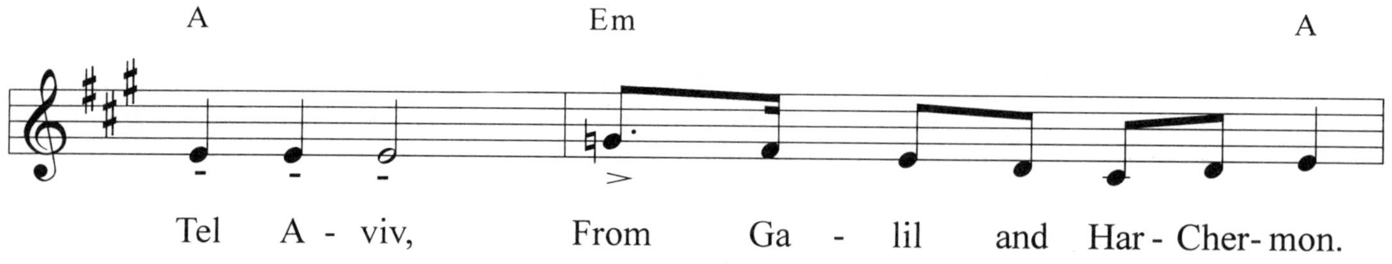

A Em D E7
Beat, beat, beat the drum, Sound the flute and sing!
A Em A
Beat, beat, beat, the drum, We bring the fruits of spring!
A Bm E7 A
Sa - ley - nu al k'te - fey - nu, Ra - shey - nu a - tu - rim,
A Bm E7 A
Mik - tsot ha - a - rets ba - nu, He - ve - nu bi - ku - rim.
A Em A
Mi - Y'hu - dah, Mi - Y'hu - dah umi - Shom - ron,
A Em A
Min ha - E - mek, Min ha - E - mek v^e ha Ga - lil.

* Hebrew for Moses; Hebrew for Mount Sinai

**1) When winter says, "Goodbye,"
Springtime says her, "Hello,"
We'll welcome spring with harvests,
With the first things that grow.

Chorus:

From the Emek,
Yerushalayim and Rishon,
Tel Aviv,
From Galil and Har Chermon,
Make way, make way, we are coming!
Marching, marching, here we come!
Beat, beat, beat the drum, sound the flute and sing!
Beat, beat, beat the drum, we bring the fruits of spring!

2) As we all march around
We hold up our Torah high,
Who brought it to us?*** Moshe!*
Where were we? Har Sinai!*

From the Emek,
Yerushalayim and Rishon,
Tel Aviv,
From Galil and Har Chermon,
Panu derech lanu! Bikurim itanu!
Hach, hach, hach batof, v^{e}chalel bechalil!
Hach, hach, hach batof, v^{e}chalel bechalil!

**TRANSLITERATED FROM HEBREW:

3) Saleynu al k'tefeynu
Rasheynu aturim,
Miktsot ha-aretz banu
Hevenu bikurim.

MiY'hudah,
MiY'hudah umiShomron,
Min ha-Emek,
Min ha-Emek v^{e}haGalil,
Panu derech lanu! Bikurim itanu!
Hach, hach, hach batof, v^{e}chalel bechalil!
Hach, hach, hach batof, v^{e}chalel bechalil!

**LYRICS IN HEBREW:

סַלֵינוּ עַל כְּתֵפֵינוּ
רָאשֵׁינוּ עֲטוּרִים,
מִקְצוֹת הָאָרֶץ בָּאנוּ
הֵבֵאנוּ בִּכּוּרִים.

מִיהוּדָה,
מִיהוּדָה וּמִשּׁוֹמְרוֹן,
מִן הָעֵמֶק,
מִן הָעֵמֶק וְהַגָּלִיל,
פַּנּוּ דֶרֶךְ לָנוּ! בִּכּוּרִים אִתָּנוּ!
הַךְ, הַךְ, הַךְ בַּתֹּף, וְחַלֵּל בֶּחָלִיל!
הַךְ, הַךְ, הַךְ בַּתֹּף, וְחַלֵּל בֶּחָלִיל!

TRANSLATION OF HEBREW LYRICS:

Our baskets on our shoulders
Our heads garlanded with wreaths,
From the corners of the land we've come
Bringing first fruits.

From Judea,
From Judea and Shomron,
From the Emek,
From the Emek, and the Galil,
Make way, make way for us! We are bringing first fruits!
Beat, beat, beat the drum, and pipe the flutes!
Beat, beat, beat the drum, and pipe the flutes!

*** On my recording, *Jewish Holiday Songs for Children,* I sing about the *Torah* with a chorus of women, "Who gave it to us? / Moshe!" Although meant in the sense that Moshe presented the *Torah* to the children of Israel, it has been pointed out to me, first by children - the best mistake catchers around - and then by others, that in fact, I ought to say that Moshe *brought* the *Torah* to us, since 'gave' can also be construed to mean that it was a present from him, when the *Torah* was actually a present from God. Hence the discrepancy between the lyrics we sang on the recording and those printed here.

Activities and Discussions:

Make a spring parade at school. Have children bring to school something that grew in their gardens (branches, leaves, flowers). Set out the fruits on a table for all to see. Sing American songs about spring, new plants, new baby animals. Have the children bring in fruits for the hungry and bring flowers to the elderly or to someone who is sick. Talk about new life in spring.

Talk about how it feels to get a wonderful present. How do they take care of the present? Do they just stash it away in a closet never to use it? Do they share it? Do they use it everyday or just once in a while? Do they keep it in a special place and wrap it in a special cover? Relate their responses to the *Torah.* Be sure they understand that the *Torah* belongs to them, to everyone, not to a Rabbi or a synagogue.

Little Torah

by Hyman Reznick

Slow and easy, like a lullaby
(sung in Bm and in Dm on recording)

Little Torah, little Torah,
Let me hold you tight.
Tell me many hero stories,
Teach me what is right.

Discussion Topics:

Before singing this song make believe you are rolling up an oversized *Torah,* making revolving motions with your hands, starting out with small circles, and widening to great big ones. Lay the *Torah* down on a table gently. Talk about how to handle the *Torah*.

Then talk about what a hero is, what a hero does. This is a topic even young children are eager to talk about. Ask them who some of their heroes are. They will most likely respond with TV characters or cartoon superheroes. Then ask them who the heroes are in the Jewish holiday stories they know (the stories of Chanukah, Pesach and Purim all have obvious heroes/heroines). Ask them what kind of people these are? Are they superheroes (make-believe people) or real people? If the children are too young to distinguish between living heroes and make-believe superheroes, then don't stress that point, but rather ask them about heroes they might know who do things in their neighborhood or in the news. (Firemen and policemen, doctors, rescue workers, soldiers, a seeing-eye dog, etc. Even a president could be a hero - such as Abe Lincoln or George Washington.)

Lead the discussion to the point where they realize:

1) The heroes of the *Torah* are extraordinary human beings, not gods or superheroes. Although they may have supernatural experiences or powers, they also possess many of the same strengths and weaknesses as the children do.
2) They may know some heroes in their lives - someone who did something brave, helped others, and so on. See if they can identify those people.
3) They can try to be heroes too, when they grow up; even as children they can 'practice.' Talk about how they can do this.

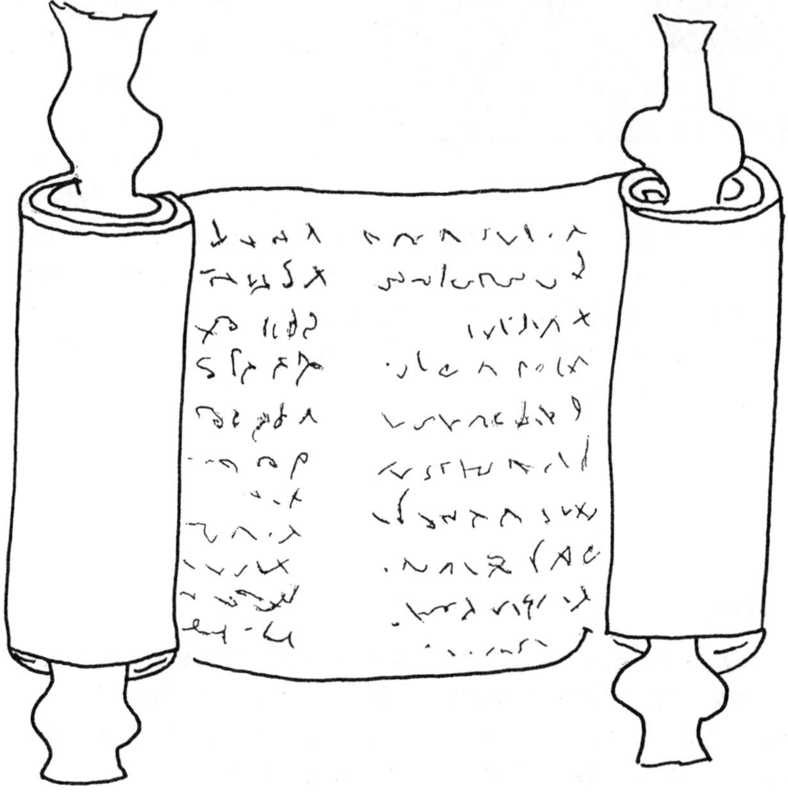

About the author:

Rachel Buchman, internationally beloved recording artist and teacher, grew up on Long Island. She has lived and worked throughout the United States, and she has taught music to young children in Berlin, England, and Israel. Her five recordings (see below) include *Hello Everybody! Playsongs and Rhymes from a Toddler's World,* a triple-award winner of the American Library Association, Parents' Choice, and Oppenheim Toy awards. She has given workshops for teachers at NAEYC (National Association for the Education of Young Children) and its branch in Houston, CAJE (Conference on Alternatives in Jewish Education), The Childcare Council of Nassau County (New York), Bureaus of Jewish Education nationwide, and other organizations. She does some of her performances through Young Audiences.

In 1996 Rachel was invited to give a children's concert at the Lincoln Center Out-of-Doors Festival.

photo by Sandy Wilson

As a teenager she studied music at the Dalcroze School of Music in Manhattan with Dr. Hilda M. Schuster. Those intense years shaped her understanding of the powerful effect moving to music has on children. She continued her music and theatre studies during and after graduating Phi Beta Kappa, Cum Laude, from Vassar College.

In 1975-76 Rachel lived and studied for a year in Jerusalem, and became close with a cousin in London, a survivor of the Warsaw Ghetto. These experiences turned her interests toward Jewish music and Jewish traditions, which she knew almost nothing about as a child. In Manhattan she worked with the directors Alan Schneider and Liviu Ciulei, studied at the 78th Street Theatre Lab, and learned Yiddish at the YIVO Institute. In Washington, D.C., she studied Dalcroze Methodology, and voice with Tom Pederson at the Levine School of Music.

Rachel performs for children of all backgrounds. Her years living overseas, in England, Germany, and Israel, and her extensive travels in the United States and Europe, have made her sensitive to the capacity music has to help children understand themselves and the world around them. She brings music, which is becoming ever more commercialized and technical, back to the voices, imaginations, and dancing bodies of children.

Rachel teaches at the Becker Early Childhood Center of Temple Emanu El, and at the West University Community Building in Houston, where she lives with her husband, Harvey Yunis, her son and daughter, and their menagerie.

Rachel's Recordings

Hello Everybody! Playsongs and Rhymes from a Toddler's World (A Gentle Wind #1038)
Songs and Games From Around the World (Rounder #8006)
Baby and Me – Playsongs and Rhymes to Share with Your Baby (A Gentle Wind #1055)
Jewish Holiday Songs for Children (Rounder #8028)
Sing a Song of Seasons (Rounder #8042)